CARLISLE TO HAWICK

Roger R.Darsley & Dennis A.Lovett

Series editor Vic Mitchell

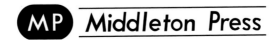

MP Middleton Press

Front cover: Class A3 4-6-2 no.60087 Blenheim *has left Carlisle with the 1.28pm stopping train to Edinburgh on 12th April 1961. Leaving the West Coast Main Line at Port Carlisle Branch Junction, it is heading towards Canal Junction, where it will turn north to set out on the Waverley Route. (P.J.Robinson)*

Rear cover 1: Class A2 4-6-2 no.60530 Sayajirao *waits to leave Hawick with an Edinburgh to Carlisle stopping train on a wet day, known locally as a smir. The engine and first carriage are on the Teviot Viaduct which carried wooden extensions to the station's platforms. (N.E.Stead coll.)*

Rear cover 2: After the final closure of the line, BR arranged a track lifting 'ceremony'. On 8th January 1969 a section of track was symbolically removed from the up line near Riddings Junction, as a statement of finality despite local support for the line's continuance. (Cumbrian Newspapers Ltd)

Railway Clearing House map for 1947.

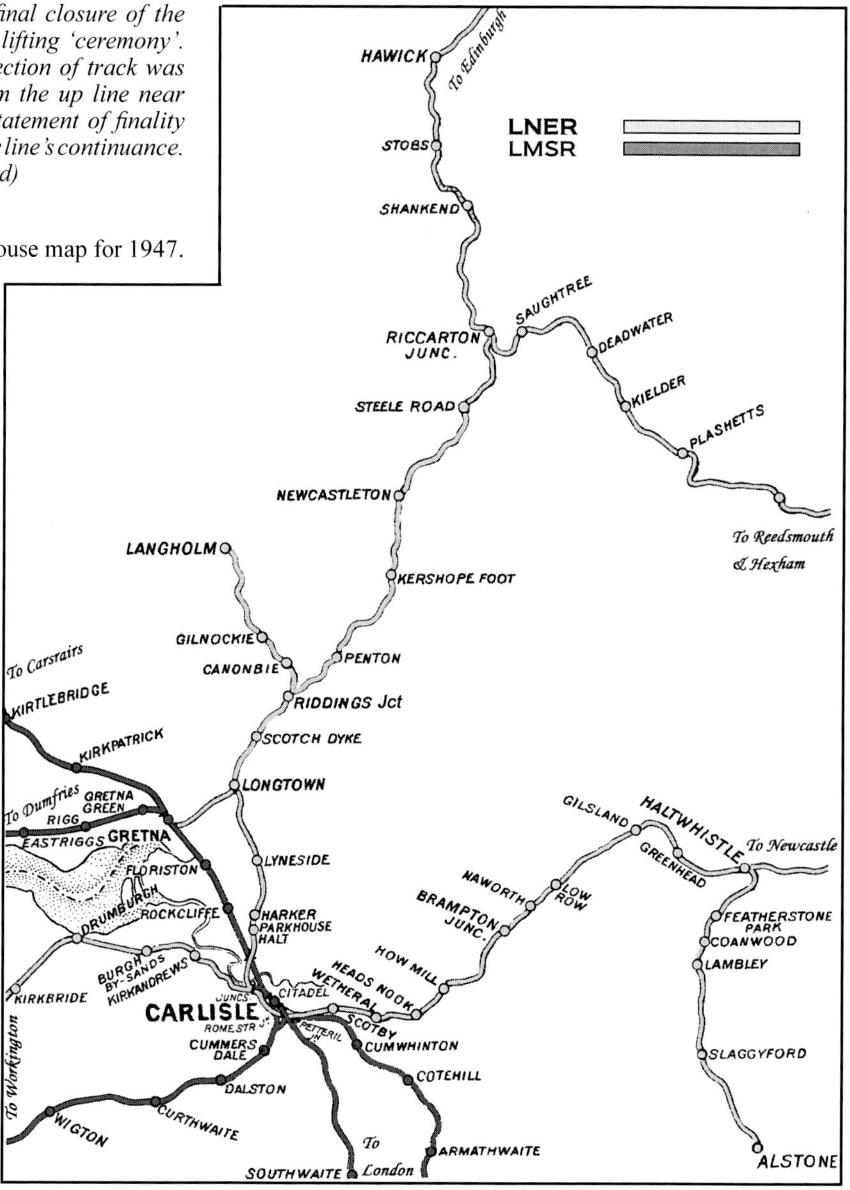

Published October 2010
Reprinted September 2013

ISBN 978 1 906008 85 7

Design Deborah Esher

Published by
Middleton Press
Easebourne Lane
Midhurst
West Sussex
GU29 9AZ
Tel: 01730 813169
Fax: 01730 812601
Email: info@middletonpress.co.uk
www.middletonpress.co.uk

Printed in the United Kingdom by IJ Graphics, Guildford, Surrey. GU2 9XW

INDEX

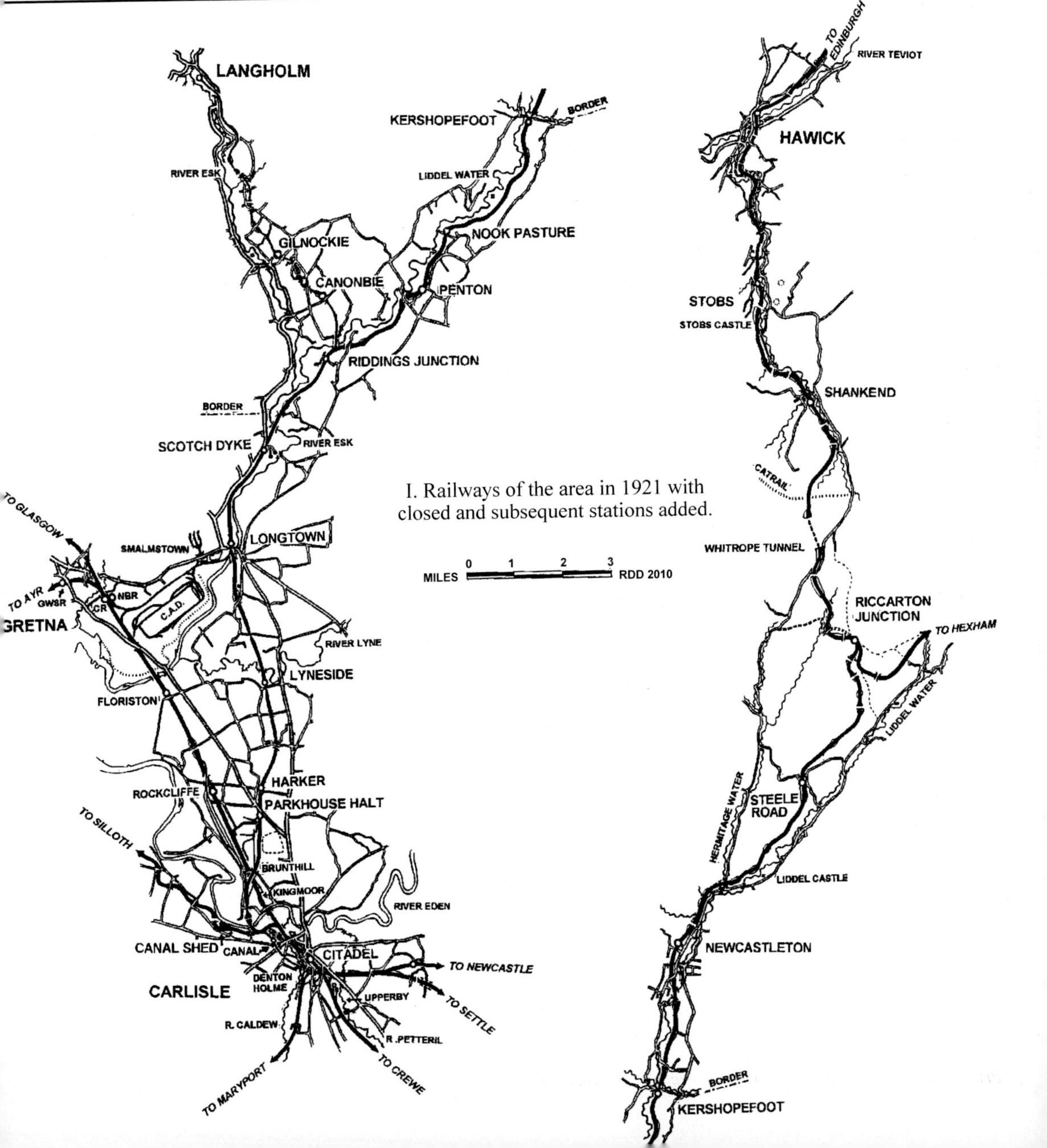

I. Railways of the area in 1921 with closed and subsequent stations added.

ACKNOWLEDGEMENTS

We are grateful for the assistance received from many of those mentioned in the photographic credits and also to G.Croughton, K.A.Gray, N.Langridge, R.W.Lynn, R.B.McCartney, J.P.McCrickard, A.P.McLean (Virgin Trains), V.Mitchell, R.G.Perkins, A.R.Thompson, D.Tyreman, J.W.Yellowlees (First ScotRail).

Our thanks are due to the staff of the Cumbria Record Office, the Dumfries & Galloway Record Office and the Heritage Hub, Hawick.

Mrs N.Darsley has helped with the secretarial work and has enjoyed walking the wilder parts of the Borders in researching the line.

GEOGRAPHICAL SETTING

The 45 miles between Carlisle and Hawick presented great challenges to the Victorian railway engineers. The Cheviot Hills are bleak and sparsely populated even in the 21st century, a land of Iron Age and Reiver fortifications, with sheep farming and forestry as the main activities. Hawick (pronounced Ha'ick) was an important weaving centre and is still the major town in the area. For trains from Carlisle, there was an eight mile climb at 1 in 75 from Newcastleton to Whitrope Summit (1006 ft), the watershed of the Hermitage and Teviot rivers. Trains then descended through Whitrope Tunnel (1206 yards) and continued their tortuous way to Hawick with gradients of 1 in 75 and 1 in 65.

The route left Carlisle crossing the rivers Caldew and Eden and heading north east over the West Coast Main Line at Kingmoor and under the A74 at Parkhouse. It bridged the River Lyne north of Lyneside, giving views of the Solway Flats. There was a straight 'racing stretch' near Hopesike Woods. At Longtown a short branch went west to Gretna. Between Longtown and Riddings Junction the line paralleled the main A7 Borders road and the River Esk, which it crossed at Longtown and near Scotch Dyke. At Riddings Junction the Langholm branch crossed the Liddel Water on a spectacular viaduct. The hills then began in earnest with a four mile climb at 1 in 100 to Penton.

The line crossed the England-Scotland border, just north of Kershopefoot. From Newcastleton, the only sizeable village before Hawick, the line continued up Liddesdale running between Hermitage Water and Liddel Water. A long climb through Steele Road finally skirted Arnton Fell (1464 ft) to reach the small and isolated railway community at Riccarton Junction. Here the Border Counties Railway climbed towards the Border and then descended the North Tyne Valley to Hexham.

Beyond Riccarton were Whitrope Summit and Tunnel and a steep descent through the hills and across Shankend Viaduct towards Stobs and Stobs Camp. From here it ran along Slitrig Water, crossing the road and river by Lynnwood Viaduct. Loch Park Engineering Sidings were on the up side just before the final viaduct crossed the River Teviot at Hawick station, on the north side of the town.

The maps in this volume are scaled at 25 inches to 1 mile and are dated 1898-1900, unless otherwise stated. North is at the top unless indicated differently.

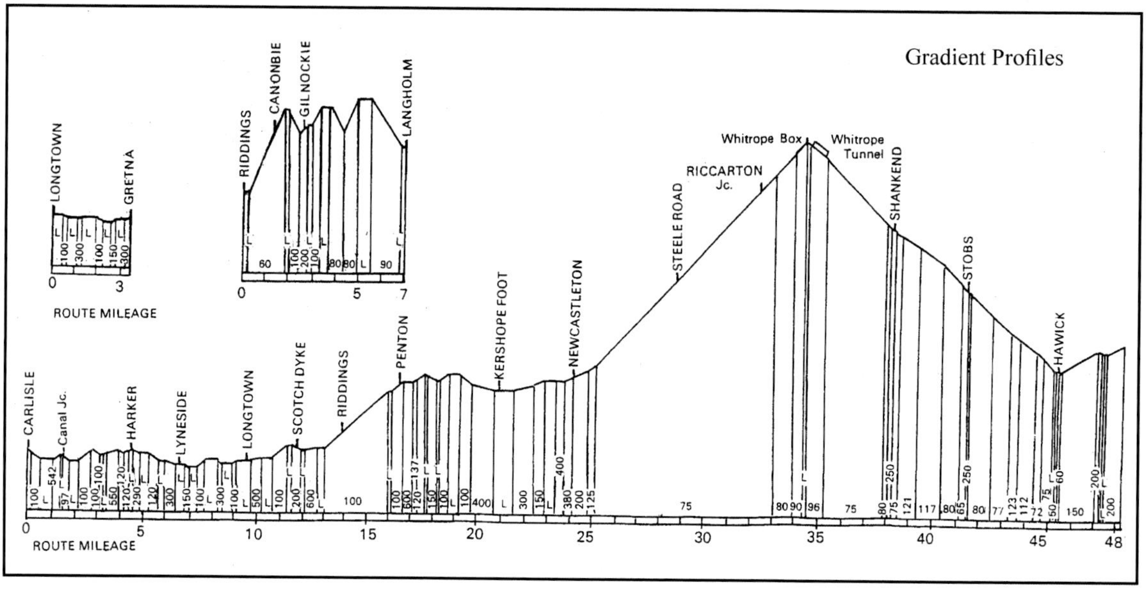

HISTORICAL BACKGROUND

The first line of the North British Railway (NBR) was from Edinburgh to Berwick but the Chairman's ambition was also to get to the English west coast traffic. To do this the NBR bought the 4ft 6in gauge coal line from Edinburgh to Dalkeith and then extended and re-gauged it. The opening of the line from Edinburgh to Hawick via Galashiels on 1st November 1849 saw the completion of the first stage of what became known as the Waverley Route. The name was adopted from the Waverley Novels, written by Sir Walter Scott, who had his home at Abbotsford near Melrose. (This section of line will be covered in our forthcoming *Hawick to Edinburgh* album.)

The North British Railway was soon eyeing a route to the south with the ultimate goal of reaching the Border city of Carlisle. The first railway into the city, the Newcastle & Carlisle (NCR), opened from Greenhead on 19th July 1836 and formed the initial piece in Carlisle's complex railway jigsaw. Reaching the city from the Borders was therefore an attractive proposition despite the lack of potential passengers south of Hawick. A route was first surveyed in 1845 via the towns of Langholm and Eskdale. The proposals were placed before Parliament as the Hawick & Carlisle Railway in 1846 but came to nothing following a successful legal challenge. The Caledonian Railway (CR) was determined to keep its rivals out of Carlisle. The NBR policies seemed often to derive from antagonism to the CR. This was fiercely returned by the Caledonian! The Caledonian Railway submitted its own counter bid to block the North British. It planned a single track line via Langholm, the only major town on the route and terminating in Hawick. These proposals like those of the North British also came to nothing.

The NBR came back with new plans on the back of the Border Counties Railway (BCR) plan to build a line from Hexham into the Borders. Now fully supported by the Border towns, the NBR's Hawick to Carlisle plans were put before Parliament in 1858 as the Border Union Railway (BUR). This revised scheme took a route through Liddesdale and therefore bypassed Langholm much to the annoyance of the residents. In order to pacify them a branch line was incorporated into the proposals, along with a line from Longtown to Gretna to connect with the Glasgow & South Western Railway (GSWR). All received the Royal Assent on 21st July 1859.

Passing through Longtown, the NBR had to find a way of joining up with the unfriendly Caledonian Railway to access Carlisle. By acquiring running rights over the existing 13 mile Port Carlisle Railway & Dock Company and subsequently taking it over, the NBR crossed over the Caledonian main line and made its own way into Carlisle albeit over a longer and slower route into the city. The Port Carlisle Railway used the formation of a canal, opened in 1823 to enable sea faring ships to reach the city. By 1850 it had lost traffic to the railway and silt was beginning to make navigation almost impossible (the Newcastle & Carlisle Railway had opened a line to the canal basin in Carlisle in 1837) and the decision was taken to fill in the canal and convert it to a railway. A branch from Drumburgh on this line to a new harbour at Silloth Bay was opened by the Carlisle & Silloth Bay Railway in 1856. By joining the Port Carlisle Railway at Canal Junction, the North British Railway had at last reached its goal, though it did so only by having to rely on the Caledonian for the last mile and a quarter into Citadel station.

Work began on 7th September 1859 with the cutting of the first sod near Lynwood House, Hawick. Construction took the whole of three wild winters and two wet summers with several contractors failing either financially or in the standard of their workmanship under the dreadful conditions. Opening took place in three stages: Canal Junction to Scots Dyke on 29th October 1861, extended to Newcastleton on 2nd June 1862; opening thence to Hawick on 1st July 1862 with through services commencing between Carlisle and Edinburgh. At Hawick the site of the original station was relegated to goods use thereafter. The line was engineered for double track throughout, though Riddings to Riccarton was operated as a single line initially. Operating experience led to the doubling from Riddings to Kershopefoot in 1862 and Kershopefoot to Riccarton in 1863.

Traffic south of Hawick was sparse in the early days and there was talk in the North British boardroom of selling this section to an English company or even abandoning the line if that failed. The opening of the Midland Railway (MR) route from Settle to Carlisle in 1876 was to provide a lifeline and a partner for Anglo-Scottish traffic with the introduction of through services from London (St.Pancras) to Edinburgh with the NBR providing the motive power north of Carlisle.

In 1923, the NBR became part of the Scottish Area of the London & North Eastern Railway (LNER), the latter passing to the new British Railways, Scottish Region (BR, Sc.R) created upon nationalisation in 1948. During the 1950s and 60s the branch lines closed one by one and the final crunch came on Monday, 6th January 1969 when the last Edinburgh-London St. Pancras sleeper train crawled into Carlisle in the early hours, hauled by class 45 1-Co-Co-1 no.60 *Lytham St Annes*. High-drama had occurred at Newcastleton when vociferous protesters barred the level crossing gates against the sleeper, detaining it there for more than an hour before the police intervened to restore order and allow the train on its way again! It was the end of the Waverley Route as an Anglo-Scottish route and a symbolic section of track was lifted on 8th January to ensure that it remained that way, thus preventing the attempts of a new Border Union Railway Co. from purchasing and running the line. Track lifting between Carlisle and Hawick was completed by 1971.

Longtown - Gretna

Opened officially on 1st November 1861, a couple of days after the first stage of the Border Union route, this three and a quarter mile line provided a link with the CR main line to Glasgow at Gretna. It had been in unofficial use earlier to bring construction materials for the main line. Passenger services were provided to the North British's own station at Gretna, until this closed on 9th August 1915. Running rights were eventually obtained over a short stretch of the Caledonian Railway in order to access the friendlier GSWR. The line was more important for freight traffic. A triangular junction was formed with the West Coast Main Line (WCML) when a new south facing curve to Mossband Junction was added in 1963 to provide access to the new Kingmoor marshalling yard, which opened on 18th February that year. Two new links were also provided in 1963 from the south end of the yard to the new Stainton Junction and Stainton Crossing, respectively, on the Waverley Route.

Gretna Station and the north curve closed on 9th August 1960, but the rest of the branch was retained as part of the Longtown Military Railway. Longtown opened as an ammunition depot in 1915 and after closure in the 1920s reopened prior to World War II. The internal railway system operates over some 24 track miles with the former Border Union line being used to connect with a similar establishment at Smalmstown. This section of the former Waverley Route remains in Network Rail ownership, although it is used exclusively by Ministry of Defence (MoD) trains and Smalmstown's internal track was lifted in 2010.

Riddings Junction – Langholm

In order to pacify the residents of Langholm for being bypassed by the main line, a seven mile branch line was built along the Esk Valley from Riddings Junction to the town. Intermediate stations were provided at Canonbie and Gilnockie. Opened in May 1862 as far as Canonbie, the line fully opened on 18th April 1864. Passenger services on the branch normally terminated at Riddings Junction or continued to Carlisle. It was the last branch line connected to the Waverley Route to retain its passenger services which ceased on 15th June 1964. Freight services were withdrawn on 18th September 1967.

Riccarton Junction – Reedsmouth – Hexham

Riccarton became the junction for the Border Counties Railway (BCR). The 42 mile long line linked the remote Waverley Route station of Riccarton Junction with Hexham via Reedsmouth. At Hexham it joined the Carlisle to Newcastle line with through trains operating over the line between Hawick and Newcastle. It opened with the Waverley Route between Hawick and Carlisle on 1st July 1862. Riccarton station existed purely as an interchange between the two routes and the small village of 38 houses was solely a railway community. The line from Riccarton Junction to Hexham closed to passengers on 15th October 1956 and to freight on 1st September 1958, save for the section Bellingham to Reedsmouth (and on to Woodburn on the line to Morpeth) which survived until 11th November 1963. (Information on this route will appear in a later Border Counties Railway album.)

PASSENGER SERVICES

Due to disappointing results in its early years, the line south of Hawick was considered a liability and certainly not profitable. The first timetable (1862) showed one express, one fast, one local and one parliamentary train each way, Monday to Saturday. The express and fast trains took the same time and the parliamentary took nearly twice the time. On Sundays there were two stopping trains each way. By 1866 this had increased to five trains each way, two express, two ordinary and one parliamentary train. This line was little more than a branch line until the arrival of the Midland Railway in Carlisle via the now famous Settle & Carlisle line in 1876. With a new partner offering services from London St. Pancras to Edinburgh via the Settle & Carlisle and Waverley Route it quickly became an important main line. Through Anglo-Scottish expresses began on 1st May 1876, including Pullmans and Sleepers. As late as 1897 ordinary stopping trains from Carlisle only operated as far as Riccarton where passengers had to change to a Hexham-Hawick train or a Riccarton-Hawick local. Only the expresses ran through to Hawick. By 1910 there were eight through trains from Edinburgh to Carlisle and seven in the reverse direction. Of these, four in each direction were through to or from London St. Pancras.

The 1937 working timetable showed six express trains and two ordinary passenger trains each way between Edinburgh and Carlisle with two trains between Hawick and Carlisle. Other interesting workings were the 7.12am from Riccarton Junction to Carlisle which was a connection for the first morning Hawick to Hexham train, and the Edinburgh to Carlisle train that left Hawick at 8.26am to call at Whitrope Siding Mondays to Fridays in term time to 'lift Railwaymen's children for Riccarton, time being allowed'. The express Q fish train came through Hawick at 10.58am and was followed by the 9.55am Edinburgh express (11.22am at Hawick) to which extra fish vans were attached at the rear! All goods, mineral and livestock trains were examined at Riccarton and Carlisle.

Workmen's trains were run from Newcastleton for workers in the weaving mills of Hawick, but the most unusual arrangements were for the residents of Riccarton. It was one and a half miles over the moor to the nearest road and there was no doctor or minister in the community. A light engine was kept in steam at Hawick to convey any emergency services to the village. On Sundays the families worshipped first in the engine shed and then in the waiting room. Finally church trains were provided to take worshippers to Hawick and Newcastleton on alternate Sundays. In 1877 the timetable was Riccarton 9.45am – Hawick 10.20am, returning Hawick 2.00pm – Riccarton 2.33pm (first and third Sundays of the month) and Riccarton 10.15am - Newcastleton 10.35am, returning Newcastleton 2.00pm - Riccarton 2.22pm (second and fourth Sundays) In later years the return trains departed at 1.45pm and on certain days the Hawick return train 'would not leave before 3.00pm.' In 1922 the dates of the trains were reversed, that is the Newcastleton trains were first and third Sundays, Hawick second and fourth. The situation on a fifth Sunday is not clear. 'These are Church Trains, and they carry both the Company's Servants and the General Public'.

Hawick to Longtown closed completely from Monday, 6th January 1969. The remaining sections remained only a short while for freight before succumbing on the following dates: Hawick to Newtongrange on 28th April 1969, Carlisle Canal yard to Stainton Crossing on 4th August 1969, Stainton Crossing to Kingmoor Jcn. (1963 curve) on 4th August 1969 and Longtown to Brunthill and Bush-on-Esk: 31st August 1970. The replacement bus service, the X95, was still running in 2010, though in that year its departure point moved from the station forecourt to the bus stops near the Barbican.

ARLISLE, RICCARTON, HAWICK, ST. BOSWELLS, GALASHIELS, & EDINBRO'.—North British.

Fares from Carlisle 1 cl. s. d.	3 cl. s. d.	Down.	Week Days.																	Sundays.		
		St. Pancras Station,	aft	aft	mrn	aft	ngt	mrn	mrn	aft	mrn	aft	aft	mrn	aft	mrn	aft	aft	aft	aft	mrn	aft
		London 368..dep.	9 15								5 15					1030				9 15		
		376 " (Euston) "		10 0		10 0	12 0				5 15			7 15		1010						
		500 M'chester, Vic. "		mrn		mrn	mrn				9 57			1125		1 35						
		334 " v. Tyldesley "	mrn	1 0		1 0					10 0			11 5		2 20				mrn		
		512 " v. Hellifield "	1245								9 35					2 25				1245		
		335 Liverpool*340"		1245		1245	2g35				9 40			1110		1 55	aft					
		514 " Exchange.. "		2 40		2 40					10 5			1137		1 43						
		514 " v. Hellifield "	1235								9 35					1 40				1235		
		Preston 324.. "		3 28		3 28	6 10				11 3			1237		3 17						
		Lancaster 322 "					6 38				1058			1 5		3 45						
		412 Leeds, Wellingtn "	1 15	2 13		2 13	2 13				1030					3 10				1 15		
		Bradford 412 "	1 20	1 20		1 20	1 20				1028					3 0				1 20		
		Citadel Station,	mrn	mrn	mrn	mrn	mrn	mrn	mrn	aft	aft	aft		aft	aft	aft	aft	aft	aft	mrn	mrn	aft
		Carlisle.........dep.	4 15	6 35		8 10	9 0				1 12			3 20		5 50			7 30	4 15		
		Silloth 521..dep.					7 45				1130					4 30			4 30			
0 9	0 5	Harker		6 46		8 20								3 30					7 41			
1 1	0 7	Lyneside		6 51		8 25								3 35					7 46			
1 7	0 10	Longtown 536		6 58		8 34				1238	1 28			3 43					7 54			
2 0	1 0½	Scotch Dyke		mrn		8 39				1244				3 48					8 0			
3 6	1 9½	— Langholm .. dep.		Stop	7 15	8 20			10 0		1 10			3 25			4 28	6 0				
2 10	1 5½	4½ Gilnockie, fr Claygate			7 26	8 31			1011		1 21			3 36			4 38	6 11				
2 7	1 4	5¼ Canobie			7 30	8 35			1016		1 25			3 40			4 42	6 15				
		7 Riddings J. 525 arr			7 35	8 40			1020		1 30			3 45			4 47	6 20				
2 4	1 3	Riddings Junc. 525			mrn Stop	8 46	a			1254	1 37			3 55			aft Stop	aft Stop	8 6			
2 9	1 5	Penton				8 52				1 0				4 1								
3 6	1 9½	Kershope Foot				9 2				1 11				4 12								
4 0	2 0½	Newcastleton				9 9				1 19	1 55			4 20		6 22						
4 10	2 5¼	Steele Road				9 20				1 31				4 32								
5 5	2 [illegible]	Riccarton 527 ... arr				9 30	9 48			1 43				4 43								
		Fm Newcastle p.527 dep					9 51			1 53				4 45	6 28							
5 8	[illegible]	Shankend					10 4							4 58								
6 11	3 0	Stobs		mrn	mrn		1011							5 5				aft				
7 7	3 10	Hawick	5 24	6 0	7 10		1023			2 13	2e31	2 35		5 17	6 47	6c58		7 5		5 24	7 50	5 45
8 3	4 2	Hassendean		6 9	7 19		1032			—		2 44		5 26				7 13			7 59	5 54
8 10	4 5½	Belses		6 17	7 27		1040					2 52		5 34				7 20			8 7	6 2
9 7	4 10	St. Boswells 522, 525a	f	6 27	7 37		1050					3 2		5 45				7 30			8 18	6 15
11 6	5 9½	Kelso 525...arr.			9 0		1135					4 9		6 17				9 12			1017	7 27
16 7	7 9	Berwick 523 "			1058		1 20			aft		6 40										
		— Kelso.......dep.			7 0		10 5			1 55		1 55	2 20	5 0				6 50			7 45	5 46
12 3	6 2	Jedburgh Branch. — Jedburgh dp			6 40		9 45			1 35		1 35		4 40				6 38			7 25	5 25
11 11	6 0	1¼ Jedfoot Bridge			6 44		9 49			1 39		1 39		4 44				6 41			7 29	5 29
11 9	5 11	3 Nisbet			6 49		9 54			1 44		1 44		4 48				6 45			7 34	5 34
11 4	5 8½	5¼ Kirkbank			6 57		10 2			1 52		1 52		4 57				6 50			7 42	5 42
		7¼ Roxburgh..			7 4		1010			1 59		1 59		5 4				6 55			7 50	5 50
		10¼ Kelso 426a			7 20		1030			2 15		2 15		5 20				7 12			8 2	6 2
11 0	5 7	3 Roxburgh			7 9		1017			2 4		2 4		5 9				6 59			7 53	5 53
10 6	5 3½	6 Rutherford			7 16		1024			2 11		2 11		5 16				7 6			8 0	6 0
10 1	5 1	8½ Maxton [522, 525			7 23		1030			2 18		2 18		5 22				7 12			8 6	6 6
		11¼ St. Boswells.arr.			7 30		1036			2 25		2 25	2 4)	5 28			aft	7 18			8 15	6 12
		St. Boswells......dep.		6 35	7 43		1055			2 27		3 8	—	5 52			7 21	7 32			8 21	6 20
10 2	5 1½	Melrose	5 46	6 39	7 50		11 4			2 35	2e53	3 16		6 0		7c20	7 30	7 40		5 46	8 29	6 29
		Galashiels 527. arr.	5 53	6 47	7 58		1112			2 42	3 0	3 21		6 9		7 27	7 37	7 47		5 53	8 37	6 37
10 9	5 5	Galashiels 527. dep	5 57	6 50	8 2		1117	1130			3 5	3 26		6 13		7 31		7 49		5 57	8 41	6 40
11 5	5 6	Bowland		7 0				1140				3 36		6 23							8 50	6 50
11 11	6 [illegible]	Stow (for Lauder)		7 8	8 15			1148				3 44		6 31				8 0			8 59	6 59
12 7	6 4	Fountainhall		7 18	8 24			1158				3 54		6 41							9 8	7 10
13 2	6 7½	Heriot		7 27	8 31			12 7				4 3		6 50							9 16	7 19
13 6	6 10½	Tynehead		7 37				1217				4 13		7 0							9 25	7 28
		Fushiebridge		7 47				1227				4 23	aft	7 10							9 34	7 38
14 4	7 2½	Gorebridge		7 50	8 46			1230				4 26	6 15	7 13				8 21			9 40	7 41
14 10	7 5½	Dalhousie..[545, 527		7 59				1239				4 33	6 24	7 22							9 49	7 51
15 0	7 7	Eskbank, for Dalkeith		8 5	8 55			1245				4 37	6 28	7 28				8 25			9 54	7 57
15 4	7 8½	Millerhill 521...[545		8 11				1250				4 42	6 38	7 34							10 [illegible]	8 3
15 10	8 5	Portobello 523, 524,		8 20	9 6			1 0				4 50	6 45	7 45							1011	8 12
16 4	8 5	South Leith....arr.		8 37	9 25			1 53				5 26										
16 1	8 5	Piershill		8 24									6 49									8 17
16 4	8 5	Abbeyhill..[531, 532		8 28									6 52									8 22
16 4	8 5	Edinbro'. 526, 528, arr	6 46	8 32	9 15		1210	1 10			3 55	5 0	6 58	7 55		8 20		8 42		6 46	1020	8 30
17 2	8 6½	*26 Glasgow †....arr.	8 15	1010	1051		2 10	3 25			5 20	7 36	9 54	9 54		1025		1025		1043	7 48	
25 10	12 6½	Dundee § 528 "	8 4[illegible]		1118		3 38	3 38			6 10	8 10	10 8			1047				8 45	8 10	
37 4	19 9	Aberdeen 528 "	103[illegible]		1 35		6 2	6 2			8 40	10 5				1245				1050		
34 4	12 3½	Perth ‡ 534 "	8 45	1056	1130		3 9	3 9			5 37	6 58	9 50			1030				8 23	7 5	
48 4	24 3½	Inverness 582	6 5		6 5		10 5	10 5								8510				1 30		

Column notes printed vertically in the table: first weekday column and first Sunday column — "Sleeping Saloon Car, St. Pancras to Edinbro'. Extra 1st class fare, 5s."; eleventh weekday column — "Mondays and Fridays, Kelso to St. Boswells. Runs 10 minutes later on Fridays."; "Through Train from Kelso and Jedburgh to Edinburgh."; "Thro' Train from Kelso to Edinbro', in connection with the 3 5 aft. from Galashiels."

a Stops on Mondays when required to set down. b Does not arrive on Sunday morning. c Stops to set down from the South, and to take up for Edinburgh and beyond. e Passengers not guaranteed to be conveyed from these Stations. f Stops at 5 40 mrn. on Mondays to set down from South of Hawick. g Monday mornings only, via Warrington. * Lime Street Station. † Queen Street Station. ‡ Via Forth Bridge. § Via Forth and Tay Bridges.

Gretna Branch

In the early days some trains from Langholm worked through to Gretna but the branch settled to a very basic passenger service of two trains a day to Longtown until passenger services were withdrawn in 1915. In 1937 there were two freight trains per week on day one and day four and such trains as the military required. This had increased by 1947 to one train a day and a Sunday service, if required. After the construction of Kingmoor marshalling yard up freight trains were diverted by the 1963 loop on to the WCML to reach the yard.

Langholm Branch

The opening passenger service was five trains each way Monday to Saturday, with two trains on Sunday, one being a parliamentary. By 1890 this had increased to seven but there was no Sunday service. This was reduced to six by 1923, but the two afternoon trains in each direction went from and to Carlisle directly. In 1937 there were six trains Monday to Friday but eight on Saturday. All trains originated from or went to Carlisle, except the 7.47am from Langholm which terminated at Riddings Junction and was officially a mixed train. Five of the services were operated by steam railcars. There was also a daily freight train out from Carlisle Canal yard in the morning returning from Langholm in the afternoon.

CARLISLE

II. This 1898 three inch to one mile map shows the railways leaving Carlisle to the north. The CR goes north west past Rockcliffe to Gretna. The NCR canal branch, taken over by the NER, is shown as a mineral line to the south of Carlisle. The BUR joined the Silloth and Port Carlisle branches at Canal Bank where there was a transfer freight yard. A sharply curving line joined the CR main line at the Port Carlisle Branch Junction and brought the NBR into Carlisle Citadel station.

CARLISLE CITADEL

1. The station, designed by William Tite, was opened on 4th September 1847. The clock was added in 1853. The NBR got access in October 1861 and the NER in January 1863. The opening of the MR Settle to Carlisle line in 1876 provided the NBR with a partner for the Anglo-Scottish traffic. The station was enlarged to cope in 1878. The NBR used No.2 Main platform for expresses, both up and down, and the northern bays No.3 and No.4 for local traffic. (K.Paver/R.R.Darsley coll.)

2. A NBR express for Edinburgh stands at No.2 Main platform with an official delegation. The train of MR coaches is hauled by a Holmes 4-4-0. No.592 of this class was exhibited at the Edinburgh International Exhibition of 1886. The inverted troughs were smoke deflectors designed to keep soot off the glass roof - by diverting it onto the passengers? They were removed by the 1920s.
(R.W.Lynn coll.)

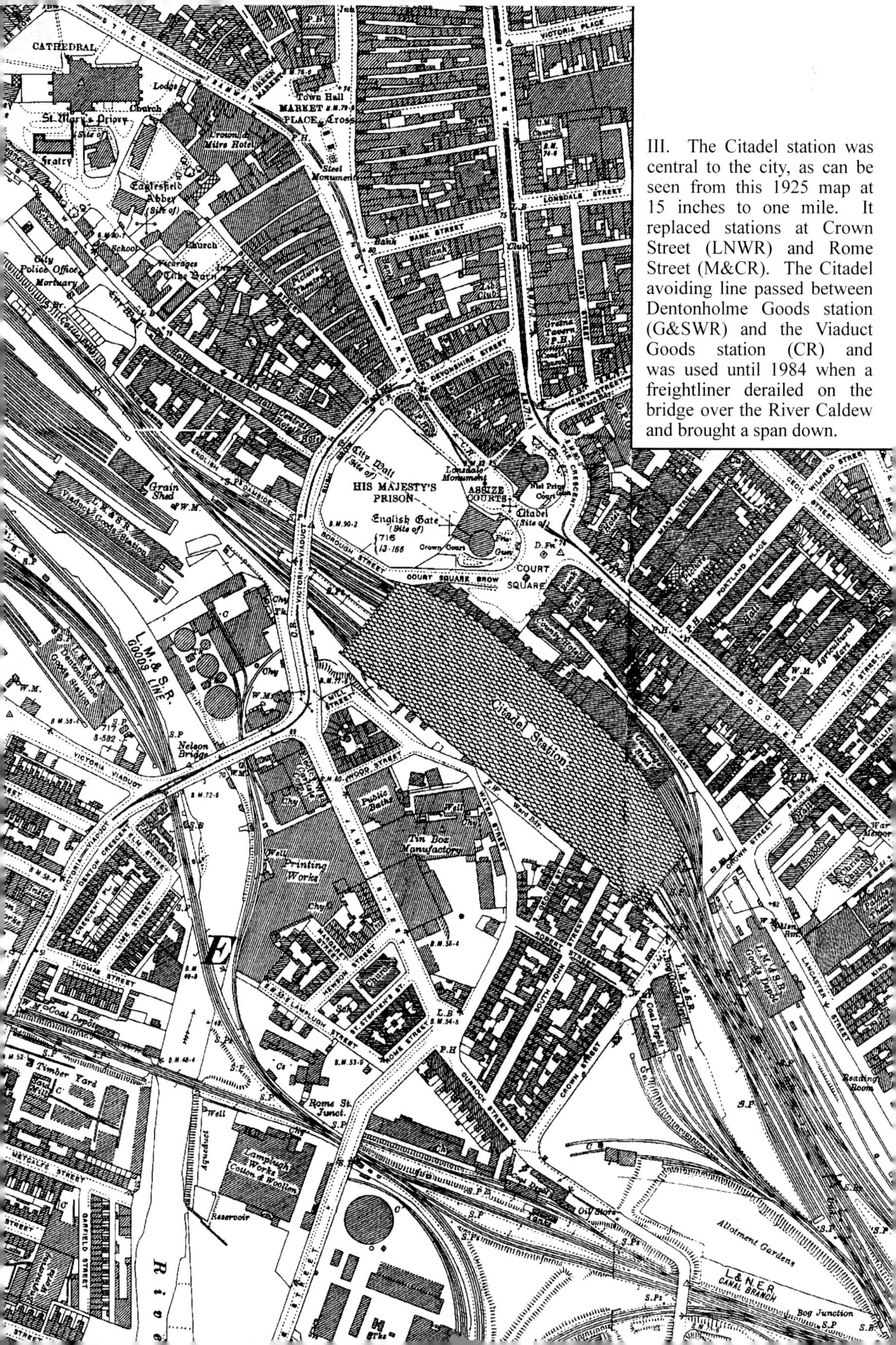

III. The Citadel station was central to the city, as can be seen from this 1925 map at 15 inches to one mile. It replaced stations at Crown Street (LNWR) and Rome Street (M&CR). The Citadel avoiding line passed between Dentonholme Goods station (G&SWR) and the Viaduct Goods station (CR) and was used until 1984 when a freightliner derailed on the bridge over the River Caldew and brought a span down.

3. 0-6-0 class J39 no.1875 is waiting to leave Carlisle with a train for Langholm. No.1875 came new to Carlisle in May 1937. This class of locomotive was used at Carlisle on short distance passenger and goods trains, including trip working between depots. (H.C.Casserley)

4. It is 1961 and class D34 4-4-0 no.62484 *Glen Lyon* has returned as light engine, having deposited its coaches in London Road sidings. Class A3 4-6-2 no.60093 *Coronach* is in the bay platform having brought a train from Edinburgh. A Glasgow express is hauled by class 8P 4-6-2 no.46230 *Duchess of Buccleuch* but the enthusiasts' interest is held by the North British 'Glen'. (N.E.Stead coll.)

5. Class A2/1 4-6-2 no.60510, *Robert the Bruce* waits to depart from Carlisle with a Waverley Route express on 7th May 1960. Carlisle's huge overall glass roof was badly neglected during the war and work started in 1954 to modernise and cut it back, as can be seen in this photograph. (N.E.Stead coll.)

6. Class D49 4-4-0 no.62706 *Forfarshire* is arriving at Carlisle with the 'Saturdays Only' 12.25pm train from Hawick on 13th September 1952. Through the Victoria viaduct is the viaduct goods yard and the route north. (R.Leslie)

CARLISLE SURROUNDINGS

7. Carlisle was served by seven railway companies before the 1923 grouping and, right until the 1960s, about 20 shunting engines were rostered daily to move freight between the various depots. Viewed from Nelson Bridge on 19th September 1959, NBR class A (N15) 0-6-2T no.69155 is going south past the Dentonholme goods depot on trip 48. In the train are five new parcel vans. Across the River Caldew is the Viaduct goods station. (D.Butterfield/ N.E.Stead coll.)

8. Carr's of Carlisle had their main factory in Church Street by the side of the Canal terminus which became the Canal goods station. The factory was serviced by the NBR but had a shunting engine of its own, the last of which was a fireless locomotive named *Despatch*. Carr's also proposed a workmen's train to their factory using a steam railcar, but this was not accepted. (Cumbria Image/ Carlisle Library)

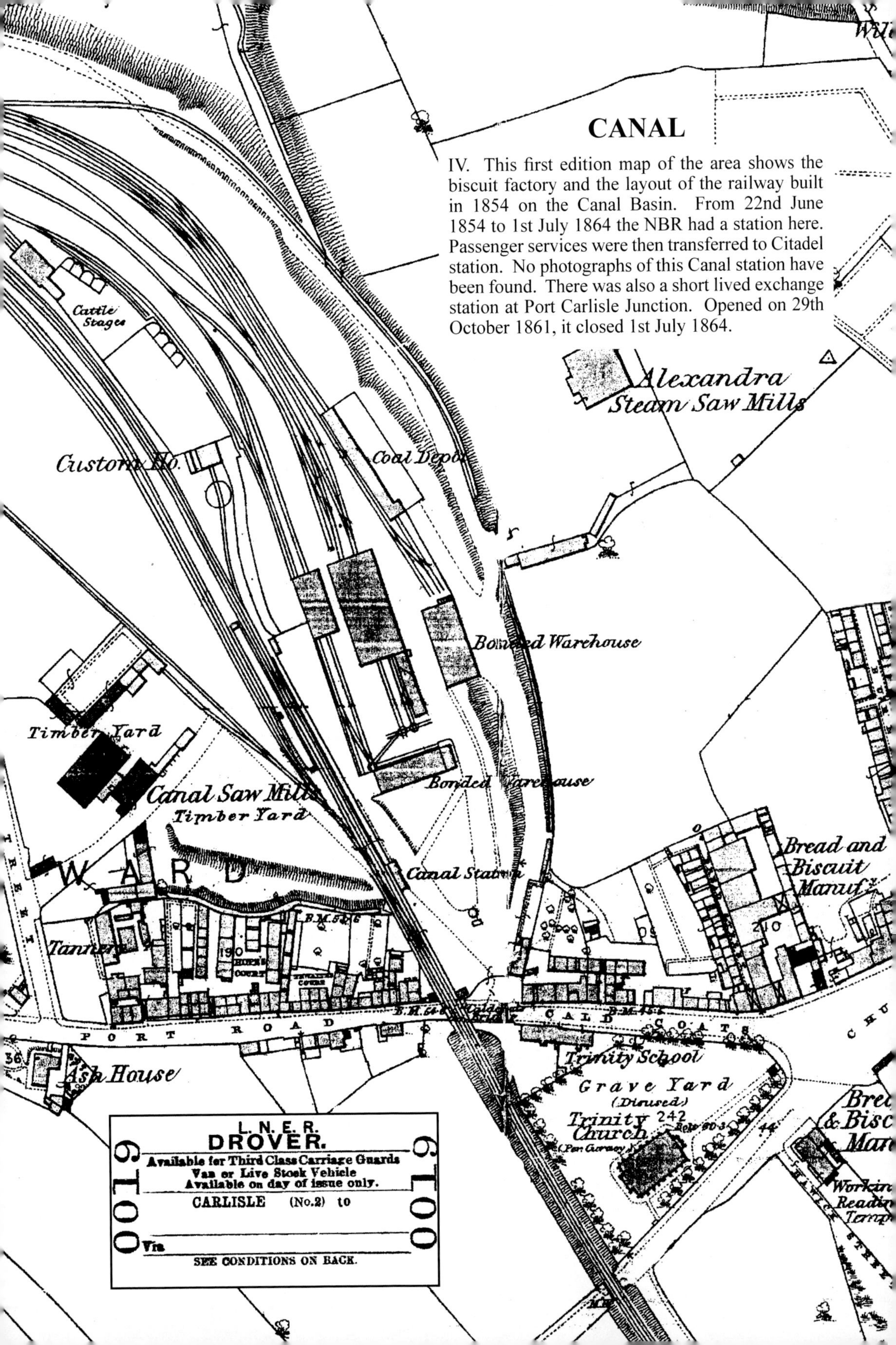

CANAL

IV. This first edition map of the area shows the biscuit factory and the layout of the railway built in 1854 on the Canal Basin. From 22nd June 1854 to 1st July 1864 the NBR had a station here. Passenger services were then transferred to Citadel station. No photographs of this Canal station have been found. There was also a short lived exchange station at Port Carlisle Junction. Opened on 29th October 1861, it closed 1st July 1864.

L. N. E. R.
DROVER.
Available for Third Class Carriage Guards Van or Live Stock Vehicle
Available on day of issue only.
CARLISLE (No.2) to
Via
SEE CONDITIONS ON BACK.
0019 0019

CARLISLE
NORTH AND WEST

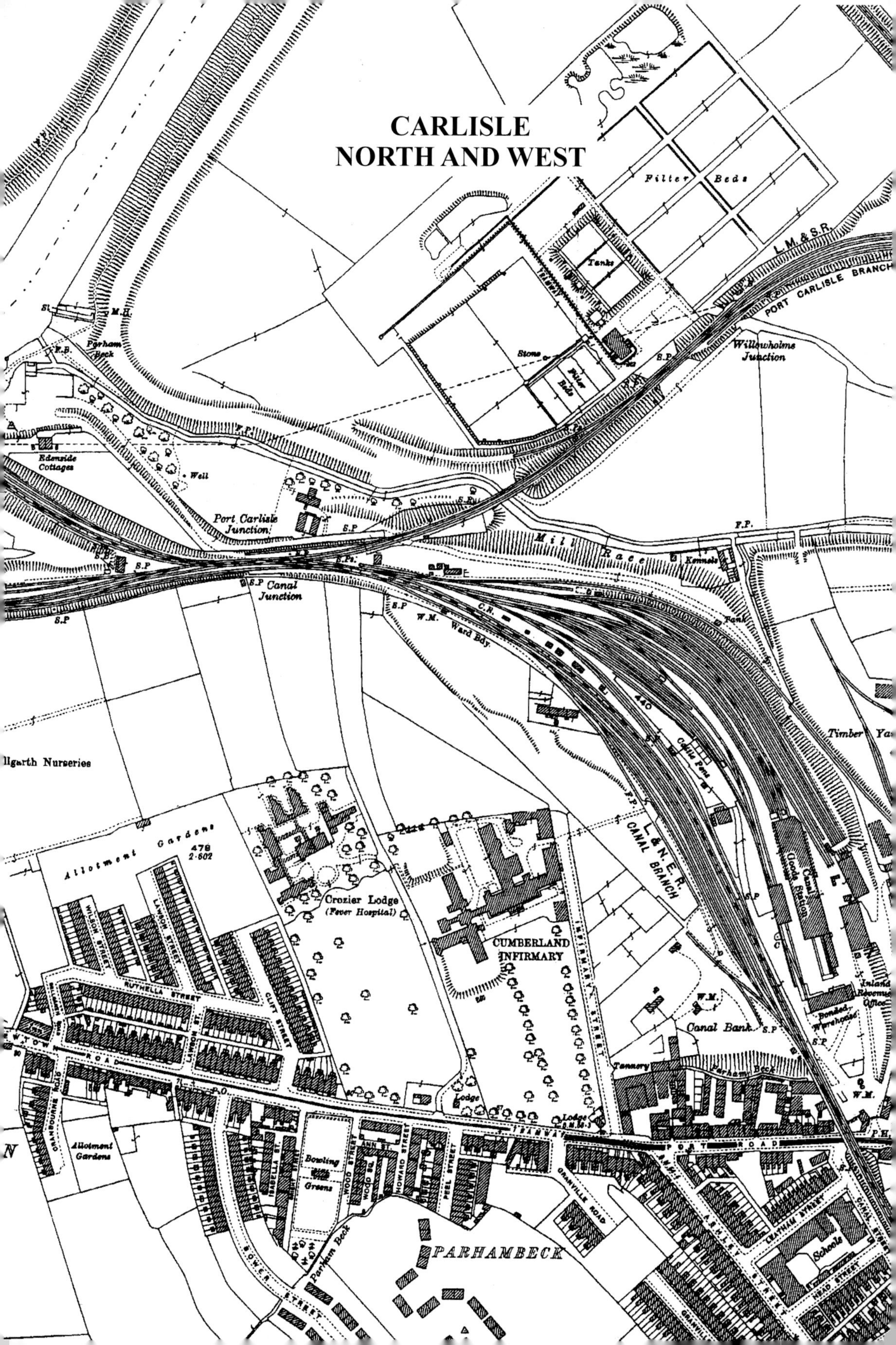

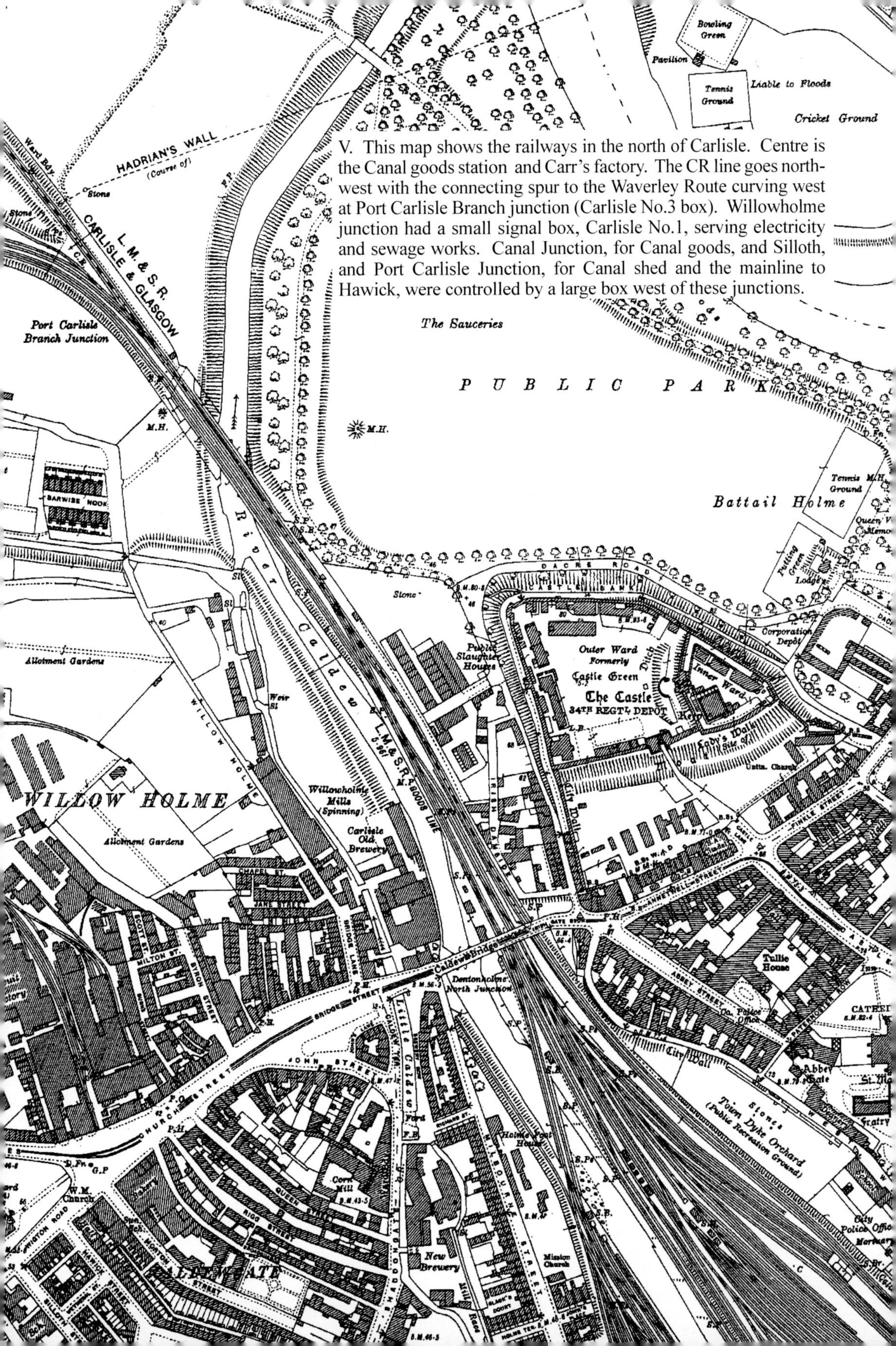

V. This map shows the railways in the north of Carlisle. Centre is the Canal goods station and Carr's factory. The CR line goes north-west with the connecting spur to the Waverley Route curving west at Port Carlisle Branch junction (Carlisle No.3 box). Willowholme junction had a small signal box, Carlisle No.1, serving electricity and sewage works. Canal Junction, for Canal goods, and Silloth, and Port Carlisle Junction, for Canal shed and the mainline to Hawick, were controlled by a large box west of these junctions.

9. In 1924, the down 'Waverley' is leaving the WCML at Carlisle No.3 box in the charge of NBR class H 4-4-2 no.876 *Waverley*. Six of these locomotives were the top link at Canal Shed for many years. In the background is Carlisle castle. (H.Gordon Tidey/Lens of Sutton)

PORT CARLISLE BRANCH JUNCTION

10. At the same spot, this photograph is of the more lowly Langholm branch passenger train. Class G7 0-4-4T no.9093 is carrying its destination board and the train itself is an interesting mix of vehicles, including a horsebox. The class (NBR class P), built for the Glasgow suburban services in 1886-9, was dispersed in later years with no.9093 being the regular Langholm branch locomotive until its withdrawal in 1927. (H.L.Salmon/R.W.Lynn coll.)

11. Port Carlisle Branch Junction was always popular with photographers. Here, on 5th June 1965, class A4 4-6-2 no.60027 *Merlin* is hauling a rail tour from Newcastle which should have been the job of the last Scottish A3 4-6-2 no.60052 *Prince Palatine* but the latter came off at Carlisle with a hot axle box. (P.J.Robinson)

12. Britannia class 4-6-2 no.70018 *Flying Dutchman* is passing Carlisle No.1 signal box with the 1.28pm Carlisle to Edinburgh stopping train in March 1961. Towards the end of this class' relatively short life, their allocation to Carlisle's sheds increased. They were not popular on the Waverley Route reputedly because their tyres tended to wear and loosen on the sharp curves. (P.J.Robinson)

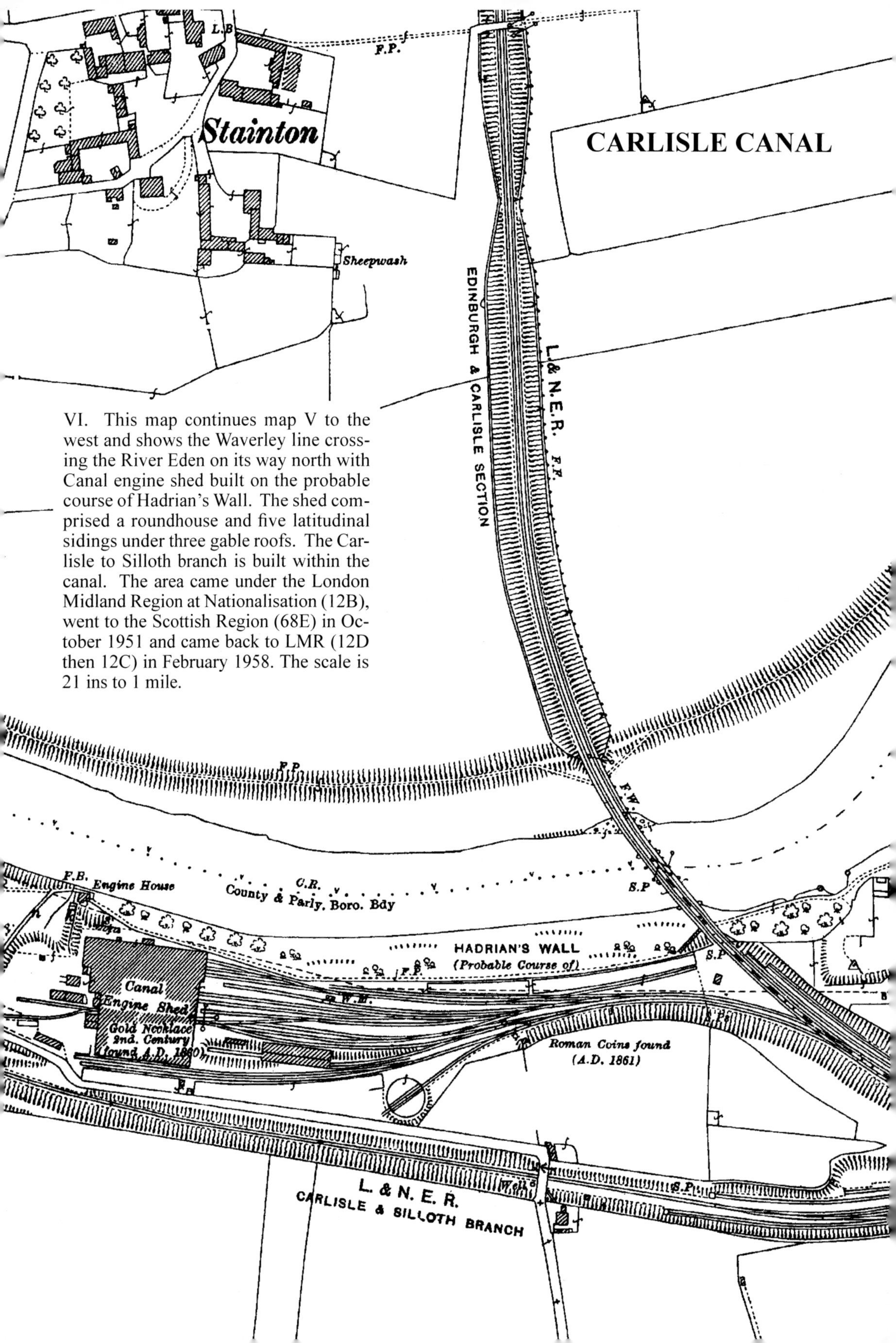

VI. This map continues map V to the west and shows the Waverley line crossing the River Eden on its way north with Canal engine shed built on the probable course of Hadrian's Wall. The shed comprised a roundhouse and five latitudinal sidings under three gable roofs. The Carlisle to Silloth branch is built within the canal. The area came under the London Midland Region at Nationalisation (12B), went to the Scottish Region (68E) in October 1951 and came back to LMR (12D then 12C) in February 1958. The scale is 21 ins to 1 mile.

13. Class A1 4-6-2 no.60161 *North British* leaves Carlisle Canal yard on an afternoon class E freight to Portobello April 1961. The goods yard opened on 9th March 1837 (under the N&CR) and closed 31st May 1969. (P.J.Robinson)

CANAL JUNCTION

14. MR compound 4-4-0 no.1032 was tried out in June 1908 over the Waverley Route with a view to through running. Here it is passing the large Canal Junction signal box on the 10.30am from Edinburgh. To avoid possible prejudice, the driver, Charles Cunningham, was a NBR employee who qualified as a driver at the MR Holbeck shed, Leeds. (R.W.Lynn coll.)

15. Some off peak passenger trains for Langholm were run by steam railcars. In 1935 no.31, *Flower of Yarrow*, has passed Canal Junction signal box and is heading for the River Eden bridge. The lines on the right lead to Canal engine shed. No.31 was six-cylinder Sentinel-Cammell no.7397, new in November 1928 and withdrawn in September 1943. It entered service at Carlisle, but after three months went to St Margaret's, Edinburgh, and it was only loaned to Carlisle again for a few months in 1935. (RCTS Photo.Archive)

CARLISLE CANAL SHED

16. A gleaming class C11 4-4-2 no.9876 *Waverley* on Carlisle Canal shed is decorated for a Carr's of Carlisle 'Biscuit Train'. Behind is another C11, also gleaming. Carr's often hired holiday specials for their workers or promotional trains for their products. Canal shed opened in 1856. In 1923 the shed allocation, including subsheds, was 39 locomotives. This had risen to 57 at Nationalisation. (Cumbria Image/Carlisle Library)

17. 0-6-0 no.64499, one of Reid's NBR class B (class J35), was on Canal shed by the coaling tower on 31st May 1951. Also in the picture are examples of classes N15 0-6-2T, V2 2-6-2, J36 0-6-0, D49 4-4-0 and D31 4-4-0. (H.C.Casserley)

18. Inside the roundhouse is class J36 (NBR class C) 0-6-0 no.65216 *Byng*. In recognition of their overseas service, 25 of this class were given the names of generals and battles from the 1914-1918 war. Built in 1890, *Byng* was withdrawn in 1939 but reinstated in the same year to last until October 1962. Also partially visible are class N15 0-6-2T no.69174 and class 4MT 2-6-0 no.43139.
(E.E.Smith/N.E.Stead coll.)

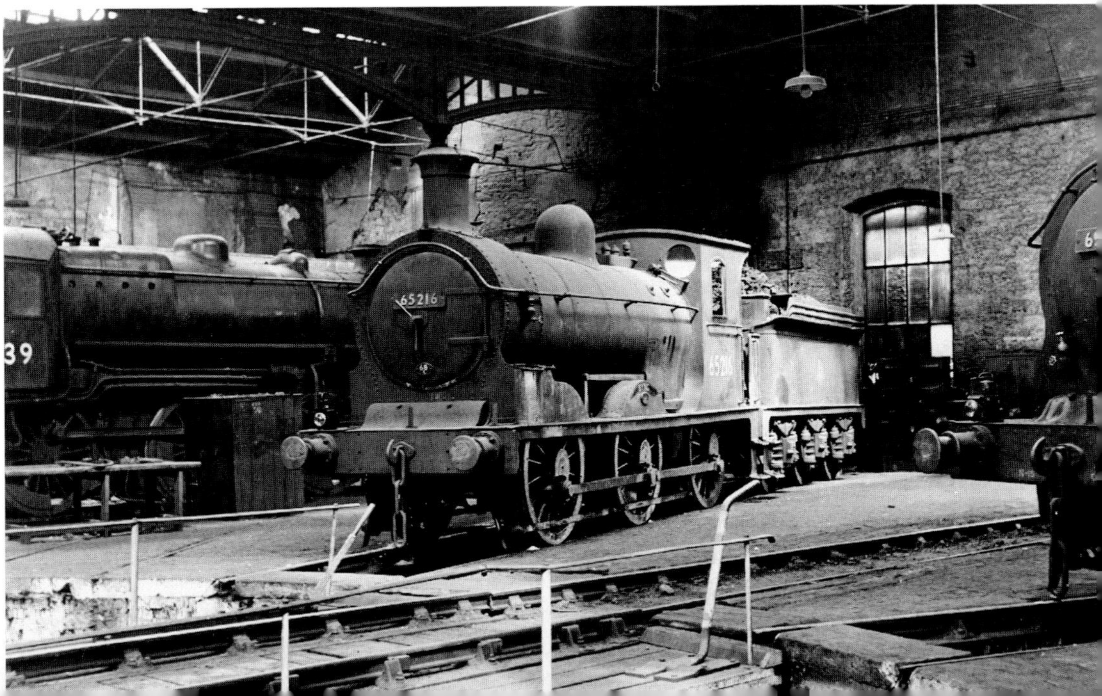

19. This view from the coaling tower shortly before the closure of Canal shed on 17th June 1963 includes classes A4 4-6-2 no.60012 *Commonwealth of Australia*, A3 4-6-2 no.60100 *Spearmint*, V2 2-6-2 no.60816, B1 4-6-0 no.61099, 4MT 2-6-0 no.43011, 5MT 4-6-0 no.45195 and another of the same class, two 3F 0-6-0T 'Jinties' and a 4MT 2-6-4T no.42187. On closure locomotives and men were transferred to Kingmoor shed. (P.J.Robinson)

20. A train that was regularly double headed was the 10.15am Saturdays Only Ford car train from Ditton Junction (Halewood) to Bathgate, reporting code 4X77. In 1964, B1 class 4-6-0 no.61244 *Strang Steel* and V2 class 2-6-2 no.60824 raced past Stainton Junction to cross the WCML north of Kingmoor. (P.J.Robinson)

KINGMOOR CROSSING

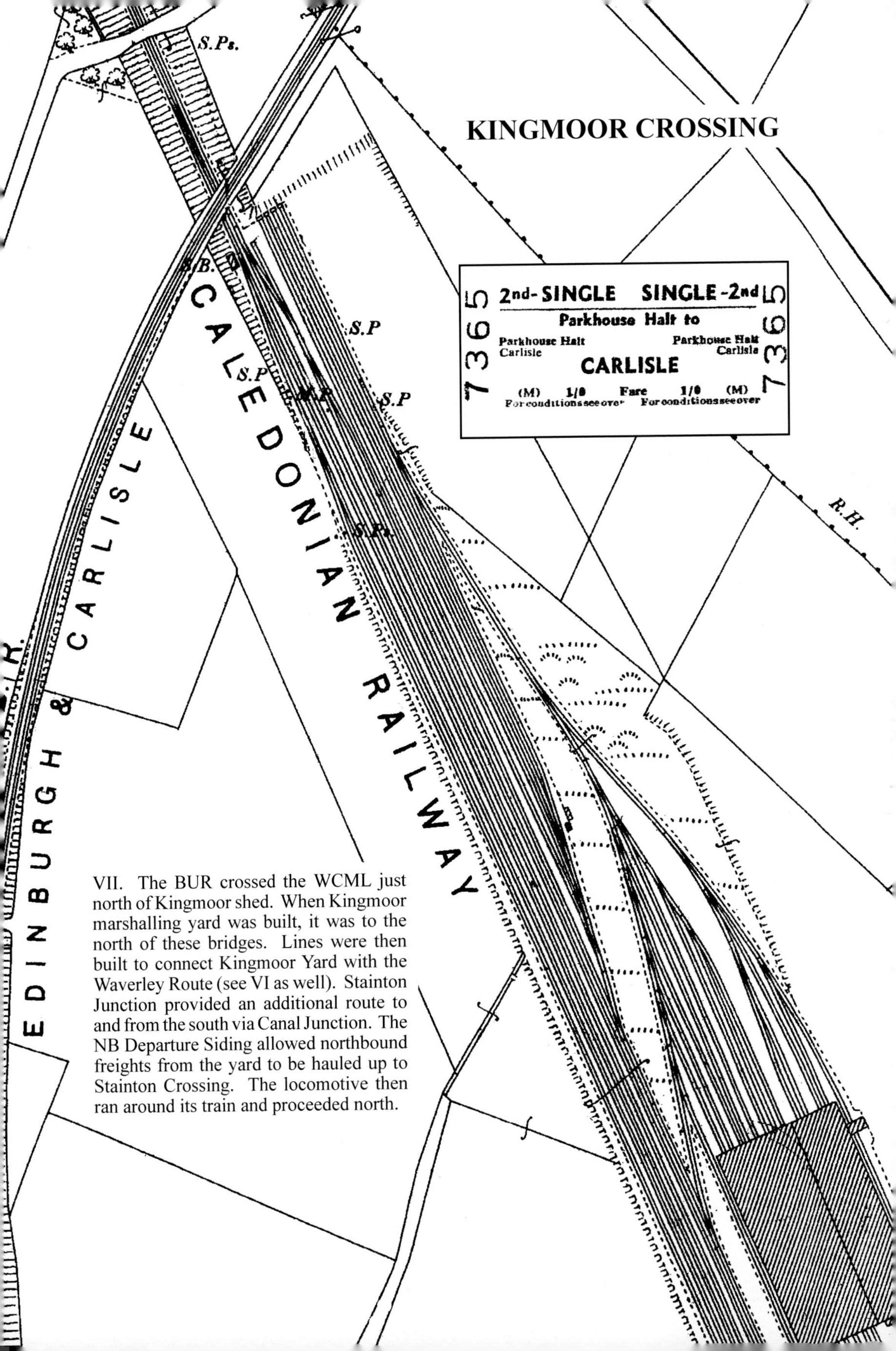

7365 2nd-SINGLE SINGLE-2nd 7365

Parkhouse Halt to

Parkhouse Halt Carlisle | Parkhouse Halt Carlisle

CARLISLE

(M) 1/0 Fare 1/0 (M)

For conditions see over | For conditions see over

VII. The BUR crossed the WCML just north of Kingmoor shed. When Kingmoor marshalling yard was built, it was to the north of these bridges. Lines were then built to connect Kingmoor Yard with the Waverley Route (see VI as well). Stainton Junction provided an additional route to and from the south via Canal Junction. The NB Departure Siding allowed northbound freights from the yard to be hauled up to Stainton Crossing. The locomotive then ran around its train and proceeded north.

21. A very smart J39 class 0-6-0 no.64899 is approaching the WCML crossing from the north. This is the local passenger train from Langholm to Carlisle in May 1959. After the line closed, this section was kept to enable freight trains to service the cement plant at Harker and Royal Air Force No.14 Maintenance Unit. (R.Leslie)

BRUNTHILL

22. RAF 14MU was opened on land to the west of the railway on 26th September 1938. As the war progressed, the unit grew considerably. Sidings were accessed from Brunthill, controlled by this modern brick signal box. The depot had its own rail network with a small fleet of diesel shunters, the last two of which were scrapped in April 1984. RAF 14MU closed on 31st March 1997, but in 2010 the route remained as a single line to the sidings of Carlisle Warehousing Ltd who built a covered rail freight terminal on it. (R.B.McCartney)

PARKHOUSE HALT

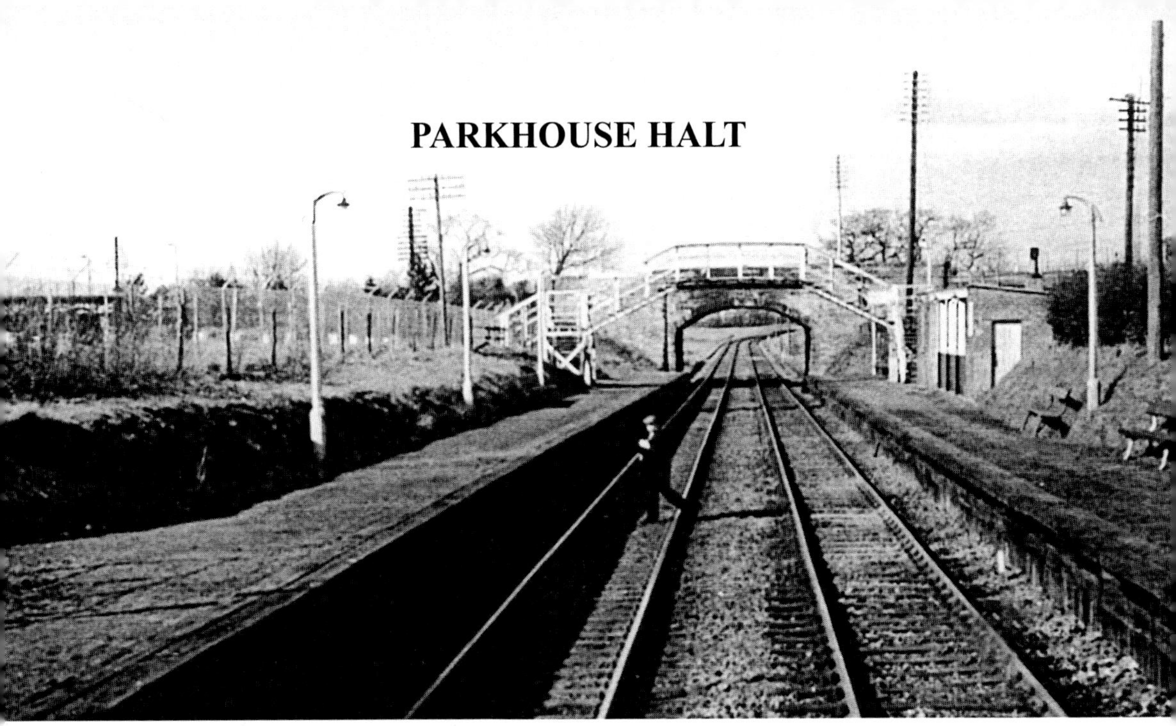

23. A halt was built for war workers and opened on 7th July 1941. The halt was not open to the general public and took its name from the nearest large house. Despite the A74 road bridge and the provision of a foot bridge, one passenger is crossing the tracks. In the late 1940s two LMSR trains from Workington were worked through but with an engine change at Carlisle. (R.W.Lynn coll.)

24. This view from the road bridge shows A3 class 4-6-2 no.60093 *Coronach* passing through the station on a down passenger train. Sidings to the RAF 14MU depot were off to the right. The unadvertised halt closed on 6th January 1969. (R.Leslie)

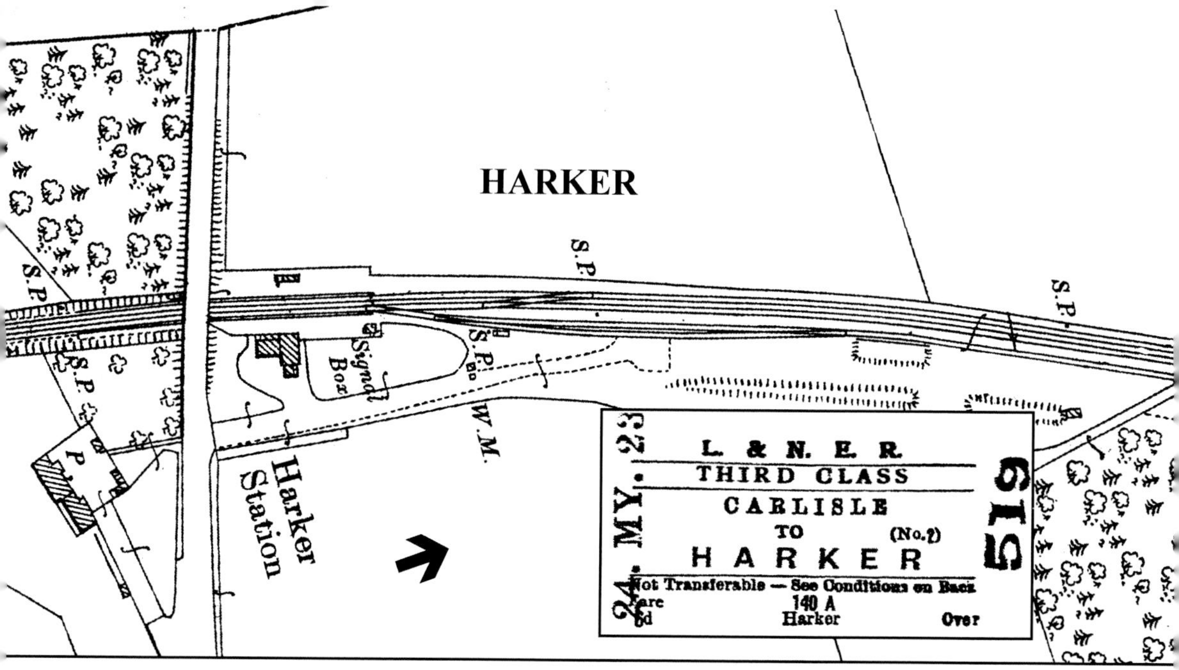

VIII. The station was opened on 29th October 1861. It was closed to passengers on 1st November 1929. Carlisle municipal airfield opened to the east side of the line on 23rd March 1933. The RAF took over the airport in 1939 but moved to a more spacious site at Crosby-on-Eden in February 1941. In August 1946, the RAF left and the Crosby airfield became Carlisle Airport. In 2010 it was being developed by the transport and logistic firm, the Stobart Group.

25. Three motley buildings make up the station in this view to the north. The signal box is on the up platform. The station reopened in 1936 in an attempt to serve Carlisle airfield but closed again in October 1941 after the RAF moved to Crosby. It reopened on 1st March 1943 but closed finally on 6th January 1969. Goods services had ceased on 27th December 1965.
(R.W.Lynn coll.)

26. When the station was reopened, the platforms were shortened north of the road bridge and lengthened to the south. This view to the north shows the sidings through the bridge. The signal box was moved to the downside on 10th April 1938 and closed on 8th March 1966.
(C.J.B.Sanderson/R.W.Lynn coll.)

27. Looking north from the bridge again, we can see the new signal box and the station buildings with the result of the shortened up platform. On 19th April 1958 D49 class 4-4-0 no.62734 *Cumberland* is taking a Hawick to Carlisle stopping train through the station. In the goods sidings two RAF lorries are collecting stores from the railway vans. (P.J.Robinson)

LYNESIDE

IX. When it was opened on 29th October 1861, it was as West Linton. It was renamed Lineside on 10th June 1870 and renamed again as Lyneside in December 1871. It stayed with that spelling until it closed to passengers on 1st November 1929.

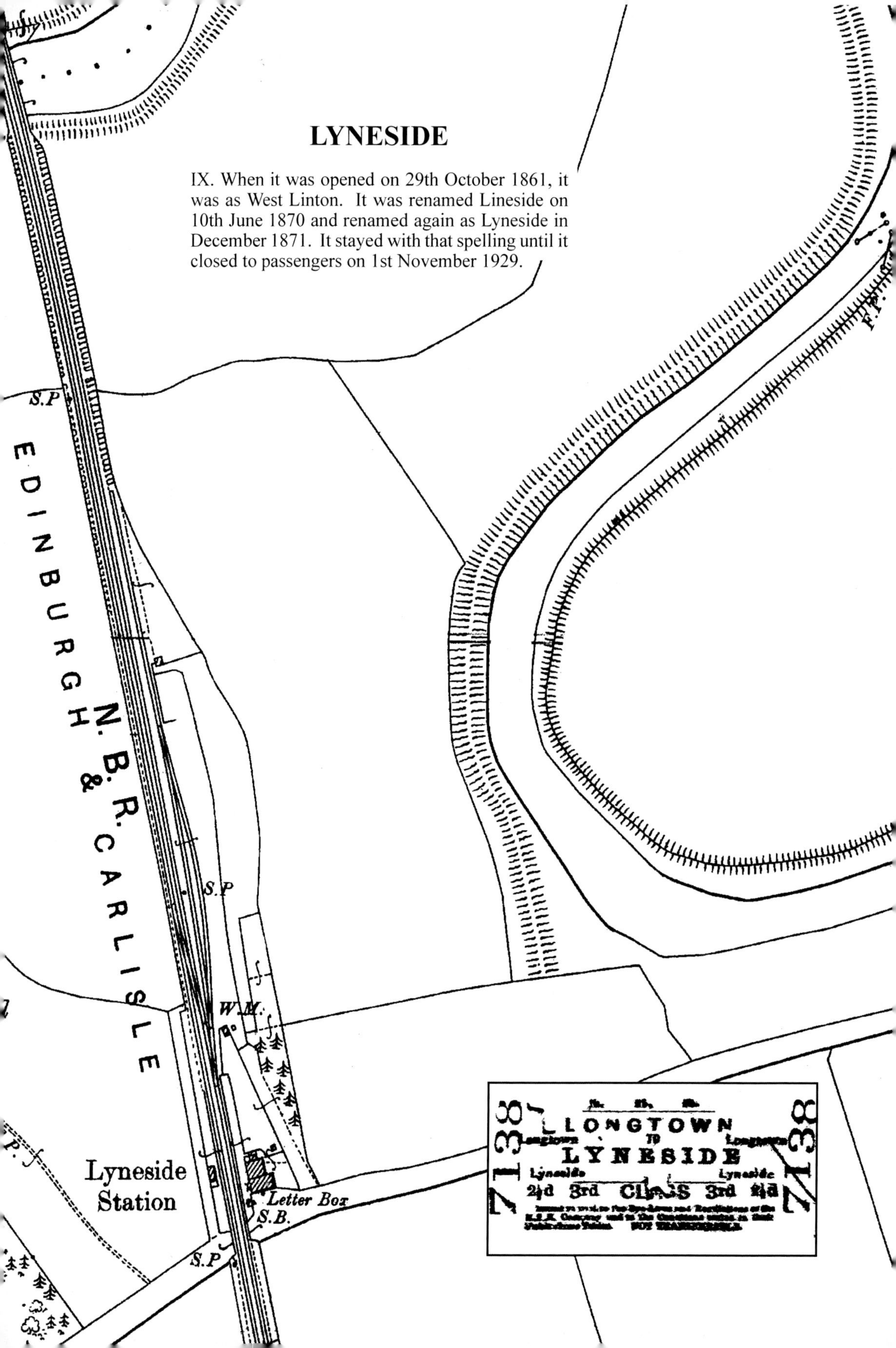

28. The station buildings were handsome when photographed on 15th September 1963 and are still in use as a private dwelling. The station was close to the River Lyne but to very little else. The nearest hamlet is West Linton, and a small goods yard to the north served local agricultural requirements. (P.B.Booth/N.E.Stead coll.)

29. In 1953 the station had short platforms, though the passenger service had long ceased. It became an unstaffed public siding on 1st June 1956 and closed to goods on 5th October 1964. The view is to the south and the fine signal box occupies most of the down platform. It replaced the original box on 1st March 1914 and closed on 3rd August 1969. (A.G.Ellis/R.W.Lynn coll.)

LONGTOWN

X. The Waverley Route crosses the River Esk on a large viaduct. The station was on the west bank, though the town of about 2,500 inhabitants is on the east bank. The line to Gretna comes in from the south west. To the north of the station yard is the two road engine shed, which closed in about 1924. Longtown closed to passengers on 6th January 1969 and to freight on 31st August 1970.

N. B. R.
THIRD CLASS
Worker's Supplementary Ticket.
LONGTOWN
TO
CARLISLE, LANGHOLM,
or Intermediate Stations
Valid by Ordinary Train in conjunction with
Munitions Worker's Ticket from Longtown
Not Transferable—See Conditions on Back

No.1 N.B.R.	N.B.R. No.1
Thurs. or Sat. Return	Thurs. or Sat. Return
Longtown TO CARLISLE	Carlisle TO LONGTOWN
1st CLASS 1st	1st CLASS 1st
Valid on day of Issue only	
Not Transferable	Not Transferable
See Back	
150 Carlisle	Longtown 150

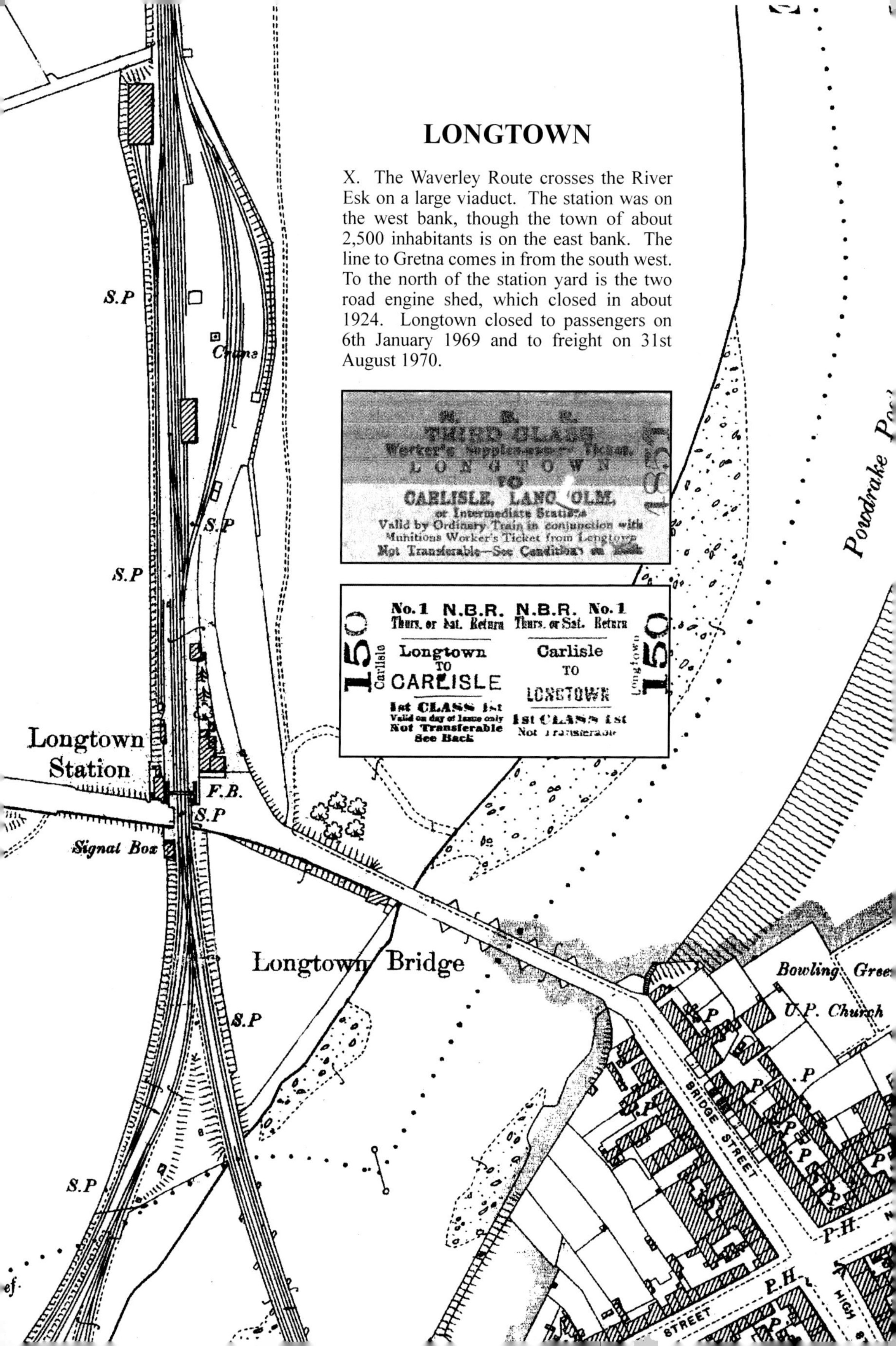

30. The station house is the same style as Lyneside but the footbridge is very distinctive. The station opened on 29th October 1861 and was the junction for the branch to Gretna, which was built by the NBR in an effort to transfer freight directly to the GSWR. However, they were unable to avoid negotiating running powers over a few score yards of CR track. (R.W.Lynn coll.)

31. This view from the footbridge to the north in the 1930s shows passengers for Hawick. The 'Scotsman' newspaper advert mounted above the station nameplate was found at other stations as well. The ornate water tank and the goods shed with a 5 ton crane are visible on the up platform. (R.W.Lynn coll.)

32. On the left is the up platform on 21st September 1953. At different times there were three signal boxes, Longtown Junction (seen here), Longtown North and the short-lived Longtown Viaduct. The station, viaduct and the junction have been demolished since closure. (R.W.Lynn coll.)

GRETNA BRANCH

33. At the south end of Longtown station was the junction to Gretna. Originally the junction was to both up and down lines. The branch was always single track. On 8th June 1942 a new signal box was put in at Bush level crossing. From there to Gretna the branch was worked 'one engine in steam'. In 1963 a south facing junction was put in at Gretna to the WCML. This enabled the section from Bush-on-Esk to Longtown to be closed on 31st August 1970. (R.W.Lynn coll.)

34. There are two large Ministry of Defence central ammunition depots (CAD) on the branch built in 1939. Longtown was a conglomerate of several depots, including a naval mines depot, and had a narrow gauge system in 1914. Smalmstown was used in more recent days for storing redundant locomotives and coaches. Visible from the public road are six class 20 Bo-BoDE waiting to be stored. From 15th October 1941 until mid 2006 War Office locomotives could use the branch between depots. (J.Furnevel)

35. In the background to the right is Longtown and to the left is Smalmstown. The train is the 11.40am Millerhill to Carlisle fully fitted freight, mainly seed potatoes, taking the branch to the Kingmoor yard. It is February 1964 and the locomotive is B1 class 4-6-0 no.61404. Among the special workings remembered from World War II was a regular Saturday night ammunition train for Leith Docks that was always double-headed (P.J.Robinson)

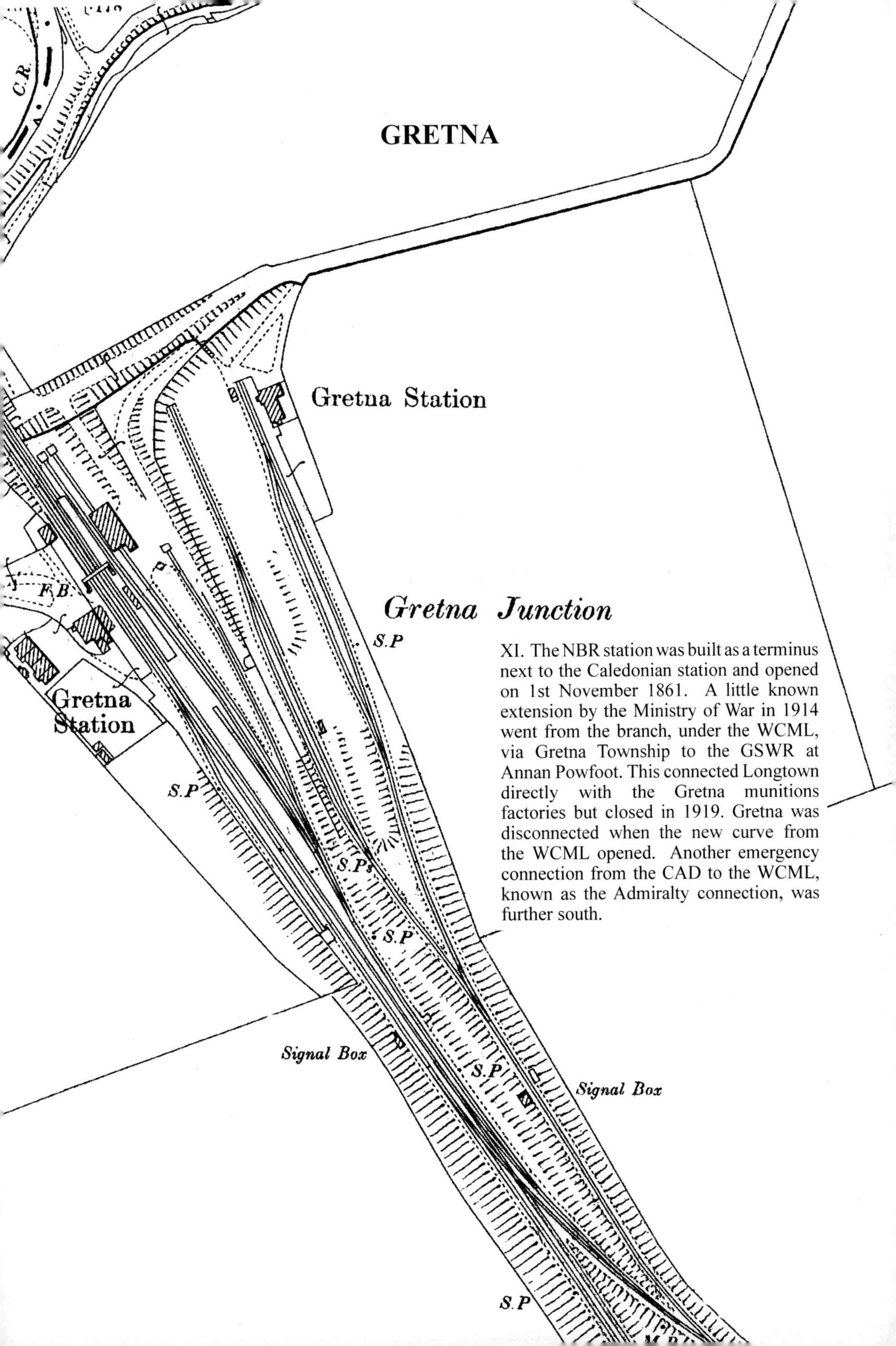

XI. The NBR station was built as a terminus next to the Caledonian station and opened on 1st November 1861. A little known extension by the Ministry of War in 1914 went from the branch, under the WCML, via Gretna Township to the GSWR at Annan Powfoot. This connected Longtown directly with the Gretna munitions factories but closed in 1919. Gretna was disconnected when the new curve from the WCML opened. Another emergency connection from the CAD to the WCML, known as the Admiralty connection, was further south.

36. The station closed completely on 9th August 1915. It reopened for goods on 16th August 1923 and closed again on 10th September 1951. The house and platform of the NBR station are still in existence. The goods yard in the foreground is now a road haulage depot and ⅓ mile to the north of the station was a peat moss works with a 2′ 6″ gauge light railway. (D.Perriam/Lens of Sutton)

37. This is a very rare photograph of a pick-up freight leaving Gretna NBR for Longtown. The locomotive was identified as N2 class 0-6-2T no.2588, which was transferred to Carlisle on 29th October 1930 and went to Kings Cross in December 1931. The photograph was taken from an up train on the WCML passing through the Caledonian Gretna station. (R.W.Lynn coll.)

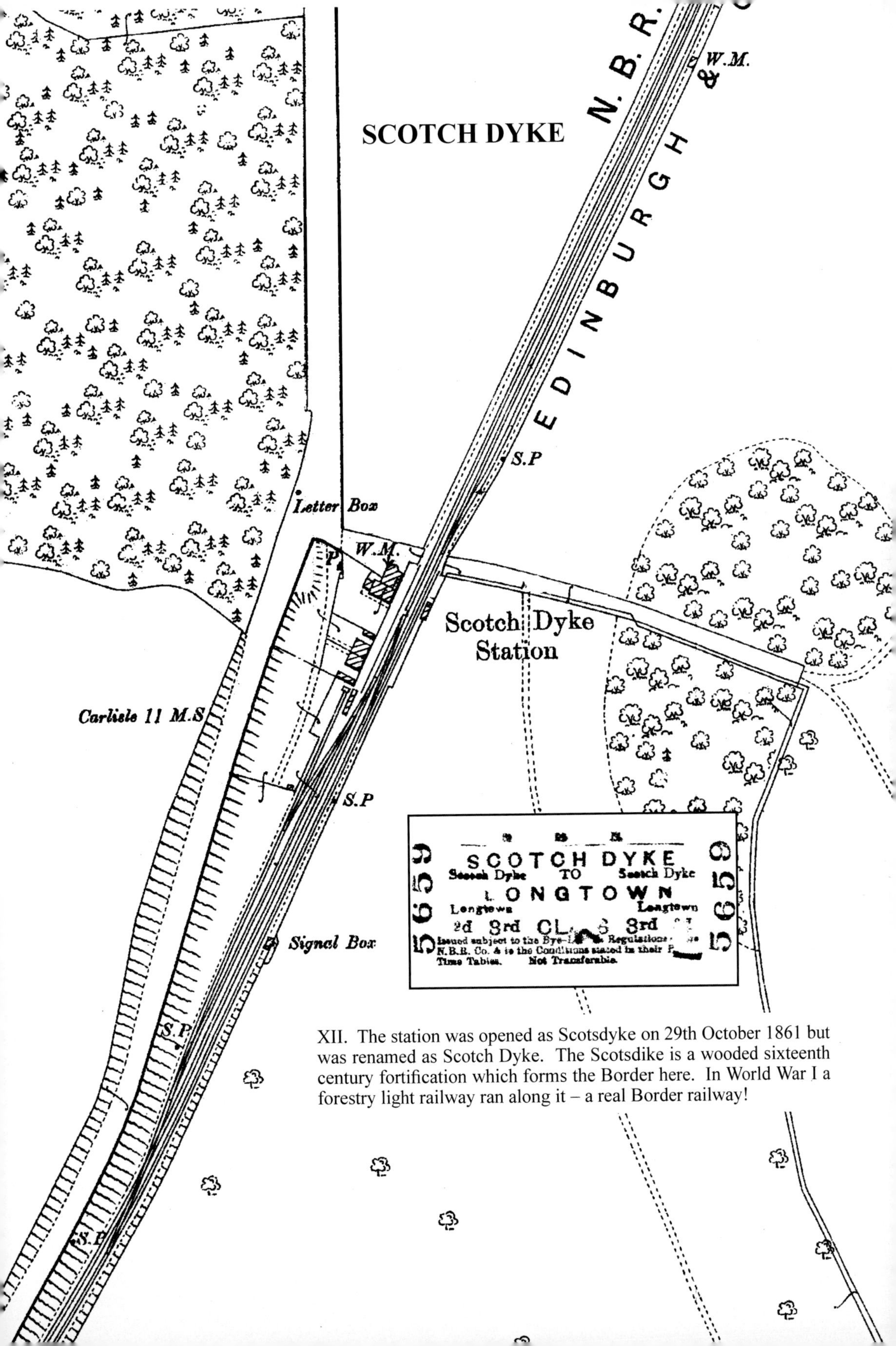

XII. The station was opened as Scotsdyke on 29th October 1861 but was renamed as Scotch Dyke. The Scotsdike is a wooded sixteenth century fortification which forms the Border here. In World War I a forestry light railway ran along it – a real Border railway!

38. The station style is the same as Harker but on the south end of the down platform is a couple of railway cottages. It was closed completely on 2nd May 1949 with the signal box closing on 17th June 1954. (C.J.B.Sanderson/R.W.Lynn coll.)

39. The shelter on the up platform is rather rudimentary, as are the oil lamps. The signal box is down past the platform and opposite the goods sidings. (Lens of Sutton)

40. The goods sidings have disappeared by 23rd May 1959. V2 class 2-6-2 no.60816 is passing the station with the 2.36pm Edinburgh to Carlisle stopping train. (R.Leslie)

41. Many of the stations along the line were bought and converted into pleasant private houses. Some of the signal boxes are summer houses. Scotch Dyke station canopy still sports the motto 'Speed and Comfort by Rail'. (D.A.Lovett)

RIDDINGS JUNCTION

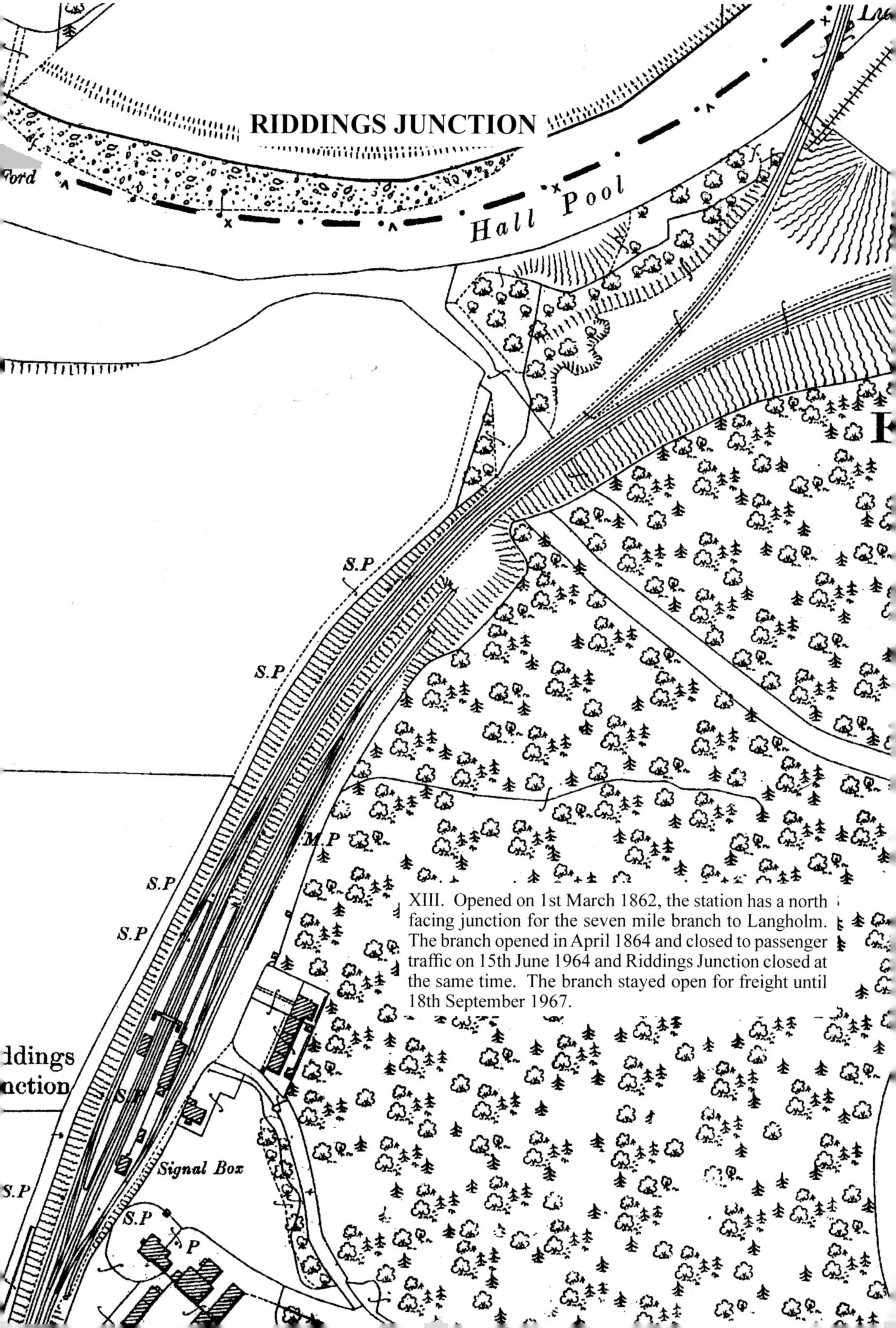

XIII. Opened on 1st March 1862, the station has a north facing junction for the seven mile branch to Langholm. The branch opened in April 1864 and closed to passenger traffic on 15th June 1964 and Riddings Junction closed at the same time. The branch stayed open for freight until 18th September 1967.

42. Riddings Junction was built as the interchange station with an island platform. Branch trains used the west platform facing. The neat and tidy station became an unstaffed public siding on 8th November 1965 and closed for goods on 2nd January 1967. (N.Forrest/GNSRA/Transport Treasury)

43. The view south from the island platform shows the large signboard designating all the stations on the branch. Behind the station waiting room are the buildings known as the Riddings, or locally as The Moat. (J.L.Stevenson/R.W.Lynn coll.)

44. This close up of the station buildings shows neat concrete flower beds and a good fire in the signal box stove. There was an accident here on 20th October 1868. A goods train went past a red signal and approached an engineless passenger train in the station. The guard and stationmaster took the brake off and got the passenger train rolling on the 1 in 100 slope away from the station to lessen the impact. No-one was injured, though the solution was not to be recommended! (R.W.Lynn coll.)

45. The Langholm branch train is in the station with a J39 class 0-6-0 in charge. Departure for Langholm is imminent, as the starter for the branch is off. (J.Parker/Photos of the Fifties)

46. After the junction, the Langholm branch crossed the Liddel Water on a fine skew nine-arch viaduct and thus crossed the Border into Scotland. Here Sentinel railcar no.38 *Pearl* is crossing on its way to Langholm. *Pearl* was Sentinel-M.C no.7795 built in August 1929. It was at Stirling until 1934 and then was based at St Margaret's, Edinburgh. It was withdrawn in April 1947. (G.Tomlinson/R.W.Lynn coll.)

This lamp was on the end of the shelter seen in picture 45. (J.Parker/Photos of the Fifties)

CANONBIE

XIV. The branch to Canonbie opened in May 1862 to serve the coal mine, owned by the Duke of Buccleuch. The extension to Langholm opened on 11th April 1864. There was a narrow gauge railway from this mine to Blinkbonny colliery, a total length of about 485 yards. The colliery houses were known as Rowanburn. Canonbie colliery siding was reported as 'vacant' in 1926.

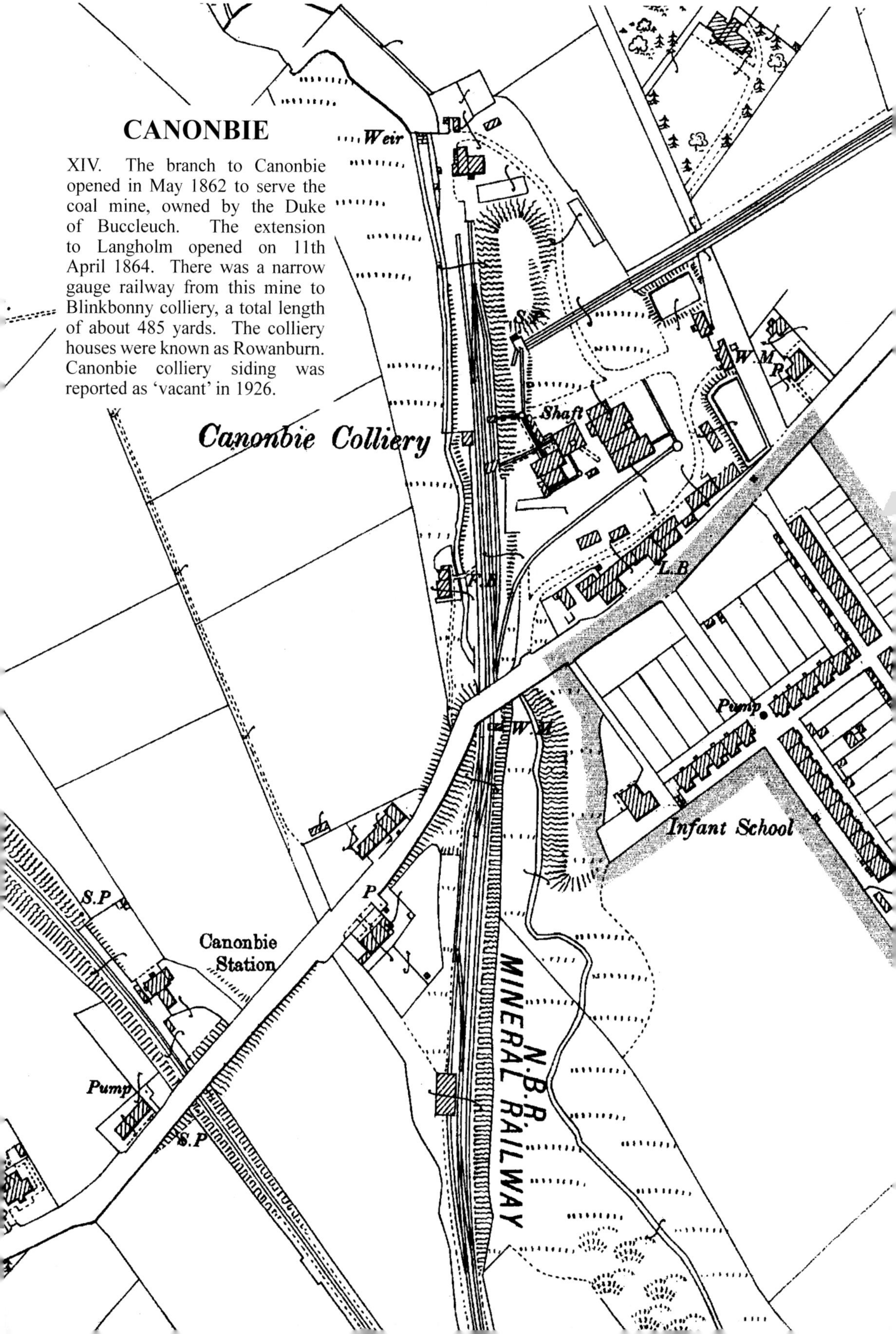

47. A 1906 postcard shows Canonbie colliery in NBR days. The wooden elevated gangway included the narrow gauge line. There was a signal box for the sidings from 1894 until 30th May 1921 when it was replaced by a token controlled ground frame. Canonbie was a very rural colliery but there are large coal reserves, though of a low quality. There have been proposals recently to obtain the coal by opencast workings. (R.B.McCartney coll.)

48. For 40 years the station was called Canobie. It was officially renamed Canonbie on 1st February 1904. The staff and family members are posed for this postcard photograph, taken from the road overbridge. (R.W.Lynn coll.)

49. The station had changed little in the fifty years that have passed. 4MT 2-6-0 no.43139 arrives with the 3.23pm Langholm to Carlisle stopping train on 14th June 1958. After the passenger service ceased, the station remained an unstaffed public siding until the end. (R.Leslie)

50. 4MT 2-6-0 no.43139 was a London Midland interloper but regular branch locomotive and is seen near Canonbie. The journey from Riddings Junction was nearly two miles at 1 in 60 which was not an easy climb especially for the steam railcars used in the 1930s and 1940s. (P.J.Robinson)

GILNOCKIE

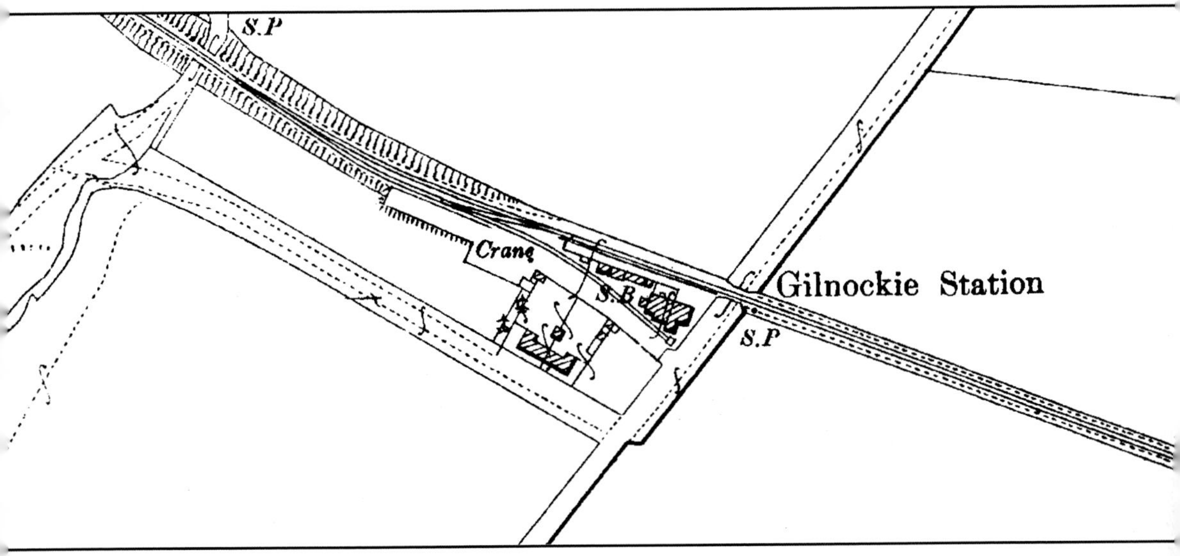

XV. Originally there was only a crossing keeper's house at Gilnockie, but after a month of operation, the Byreburn viaduct became unstable. For a few days passengers walked across the nine-arch viaduct to meet trains and continue their journey. Then the Langholm road coach had six months further service while repairs were carried out. During this period the NBR decided to build the station.

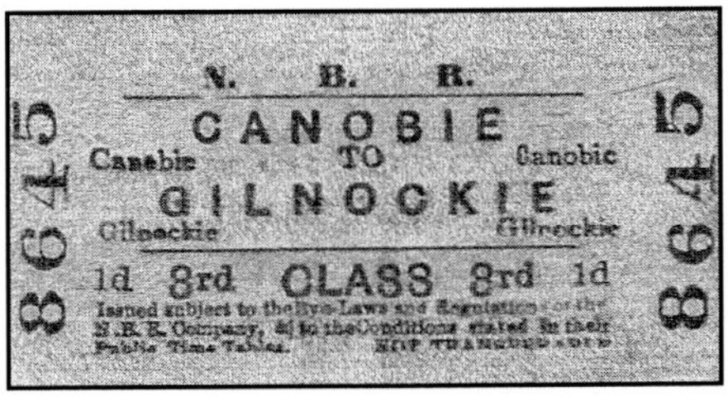

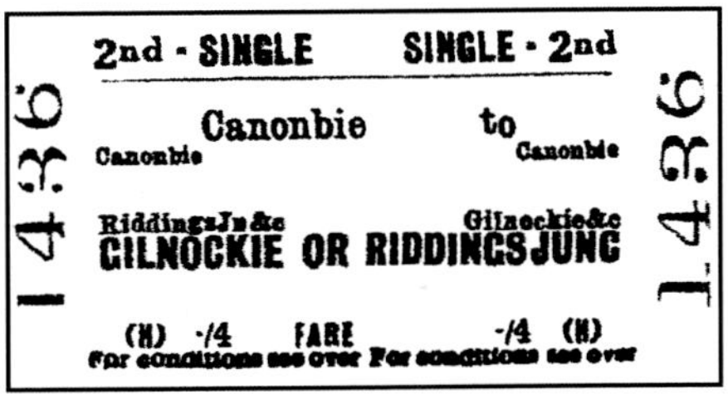

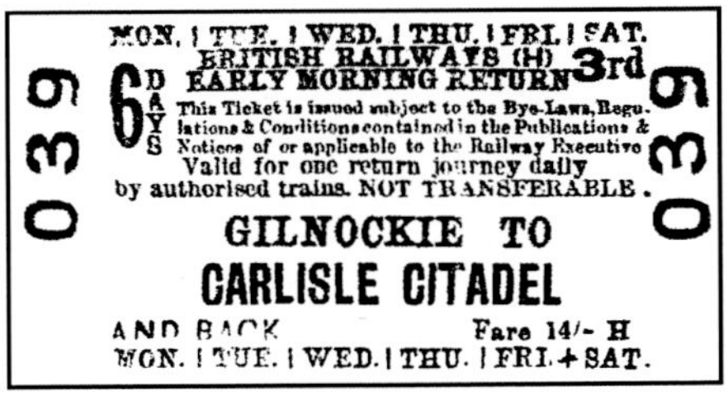

51. The station opened on 2nd November 1864. Passenger traffic was never heavy and passenger facilities rather basic, though the floral display was always good. World War II brought Canadian foresters to the area and the siding was often filled with bogie bolster wagons of timber. From the turn of the century, the station appeared in the timetables as Gilnockie for Claygate. (Stations UK)

52. This view is looking back towards Canonbie. Gilnockie's busiest day was 'Simmer Fair Nicht', when it became the custom for exiles returning to Langholm for the Common Riding to go to Gilnockie and catch the train to Langholm, where they would be met by the Flute Band and piped around the town. It was an unstaffed halt from 2nd February 1953 until closure. (Stations UK)

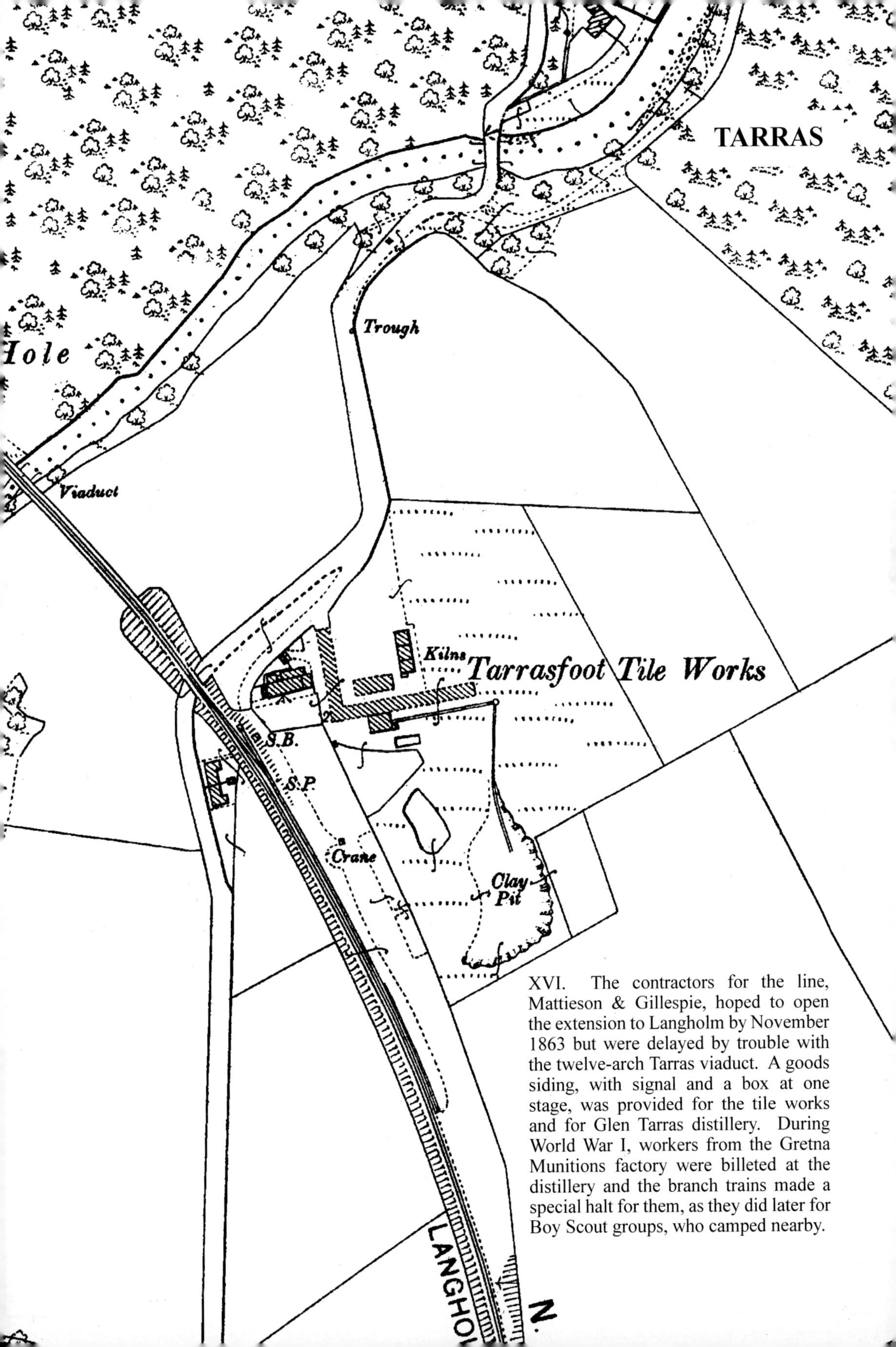

XVI. The contractors for the line, Mattieson & Gillespie, hoped to open the extension to Langholm by November 1863 but were delayed by trouble with the twelve-arch Tarras viaduct. A goods siding, with signal and a box at one stage, was provided for the tile works and for Glen Tarras distillery. During World War I, workers from the Gretna Munitions factory were billeted at the distillery and the branch trains made a special halt for them, as they did later for Boy Scout groups, who camped nearby.

53. Before the closure of the branch, there were several visiting specials. Here the SLS/MLS Carlisle Rail Tour hauled by restored class D34 4-4-0 no.256 *Glen Douglas* is crossing the Tarras viaduct on its way back from Langholm on 6th April 1963. The locomotive in 2010 was at the Scottish Railway Preservation Society, Bo'ness, but both Tarras and Byreburn viaducts were demolished in 1986. (G.W.Morrison)

1937 Working Timetable.

LANGHOLM BRANCH.

DOWN TRAINS.	Distance from Riddings.		WEEK-DAYS. 1	2	3‡	4‡	5	7	8	9	11	12	14	15	17	18
			Goods	O.P.	O.P. Steam Coach	O.P. Steam Coach	Goods	§	O.P. Steam Coach	O.P.	O.P. Steam Coach	O.P.	O.P.	O.P. Steam Coach	O.P.	O.P.
CLASS			D	...	...	...	D	...	...	...	...	...	...	...	...	...
Departs from ...			*Carlisle* a.m. 5 57	...	*Carlisle* a.m. 9 20	*Carlisle* a.m. 9 33	*Longtown* a.m. 10 5	...	*Carlisle* p.m. 1 20	*Carlisle* p.m. 1 31	*Carlisle* p.m. 4 42	*Carlisle* p.m. 4 50	*Carlisle* p.m. 8 16	*Carlisle* p.m. 8 16	...	*Carlisle* p.m. 11 5
									SX	SOZ	SXZ	SOZ	SOZ	SXZ	SOZ	SO
	M.	C.	a.m.	a.m.	a.m.	a.m.	a.m.	p.m.	p.m.	p.m.	p.m.	p.m.	p.m.	p.m	p.m.	p.m.
—Riddings Junction ...dep.	...	...	6 28	7 47	9 52	10 5	10 25	12 36	1 52	1 56	5 13	5 17	8 42	8 47	9 40	11 30
Canonbie ... ... "	1	29	......	7 51	9 57	10 10	RV	......	1 57	2 0	5 19	5 21	8 46	8 53	9 45	11 34
Gilnockie (for Claygate) "	2	62	...	7 55	10 1	10 14	10 42	...	2 1	2 4	5 25	5 25	8 50	8 59	9 49	11 38
Glentarras Siding arr.	4	48	......	......	......	......	......	......	......	......	......	......	......	......	......	......
Glentarras Siding dep.	...	...	...	...	...	...	...	...	...	...	...	...	...	...	...	...
—Langholm ... ... arr.	7	8	6 52	8 4	10 10	10 23	10 51	12 51	2 10	2 13	5 34	5 34	8 59	9 8	9 58	11 47

UP TRAINS.	Distance from Langholm.		WEEK-DAYS. 24‡	25	26‡	27‡	28	30	31	32	34	35	37	38	40	42
			O.P. Mixed	O.P.	O.P. Steam Coach	O.P. Steam Coach	Goods	O.P.	O.P. Steam Coach	O.P.	O.P. Steam Coach	O.P.	O.P. Steam Coach	O.P.	O.P.	E.C.S.
CLASS			...	...	...	...	D	...	...	...	...	...	...	...	...	...
			Z			SO		Z	SXZ	SO	SXZ	SO	SX	SO	SO	SO
	M.	C.	a.m.	a.m.	a.m.	a.m.	a.m.	p.m.	p.m.	p.m.	p.m.	p.m.	p.m.	p.m.	p.m.	p.m.
—Langholm ... ...dep.	...	...	7 15	8 52	10 55	11 0	11 40	12 59	3 28	3 28	6 0	6 3	9 12	9 18	10 8	11 55
Glentarras Siding arr.	2	40	......	......	......	......	......	......	......	......	......	......	......	......	......	......
Glentarras Siding dep.	...	...	...	...	...	...	...	...	...	...	...	...	...	...	...	...
Gilnockie (for Claygate) "	4	26	7 25	9 1	11 6	11 11	12 8	1 8	3 39	3 37	6 11	6 12	9 23	9 27	10 17	......
Canonbie ... ... "	5	59	7 30	9 5	11 11	11 16	12 18	1 12	3 44	3 42	6 16	6 17	9 28	9 31	10 21	...
—Riddings Junction ... arr.	7	8	7 34	9 9	11 15	11 20	12 28	1 16	3 48	3 46	6 20	6 20	9 32	9 35	10 25	12 11
Arrives at	...	...	...	*Longtown* 9 30 E. & V.	*Carlisle* a.m. 11 45	*Carlisle* a.m. 11 50	...	*Carlisle* p.m. 1 42 SX	*Carlisle* 4 22	*Carlisle* 4 15	*Carlisle* 6 52	*Carlisle* 6 52	*Carlisle* 10 1	...	*Carlisle* 10 51	*Canal Sheds* 12 35

No. 3.—‡ Runs until May 31 and from September 20.

No. 4.—‡ Runs from June 1 to September 18 inclusive.

No. 5.—Traffic for Gilnockie to be taken forward to Langholm and returned by 11.40 a.m. Goods.

No. 24.—‡ Three additional minutes to be allowed when an attachment is made at Gilnockie, and five minutes when an attachment is made at Canonbie.

No. 26.—‡ Saturdays excepted after July 3.

No. 27.—‡ Saturdays only. Commences July 10.

GRETNA BRANCH.

DOWN TRAINS.	Distance from Gretna.		WEEK-DAYS 1	3
			Goods	
CLASS			D	...
Departs from ...			*Carlisle* a.m. 8 10	...
	M.	C.	a.m.	
Gretna (L. & N.E.) ...dep.	...	...	10 15	...
—Longtown Junction ... arr.	3	17	10 25	......
Arrives at			*Carlisle* (*Can.*) 11 §20 SX 2SO §0	...

UP TRAINS.	Distance from Longtown.		WEEK-DAYS 4	5
			Goods	
CLASS			D	...
Departs from ...			*Carlisle* a.m. 8 10	...
	M.	C.	a.m.	
—Longtown Junction ...dep.	...	...	9 2	...
Gretna (L. & N.E.) .. arr.	3	17	9 15	......
Arrives at			*Carlisle* (*Can.*) 11 §20 SX 2SO §0	...

No. 1.—After arrival Longtown Light Engine and Guard will leave at 11.0 a.m. SX for Carlisle (Canal), arriving there 11.20 a.m., and take up working of 11.35 a.m. Goods, Carlisle (Canal) to Silloth, Traffic left off at Longtown must be marshalled on Brake Van ready for catch-on by 6.50 a.m. Goods ex Carlisle on return.

LANGHOLM

XVII. The well equipped terminus was central for the woollen mills and the town of 3,500 people. The turntable, in front of the engine shed, was removed in the first World War. The shed itself closed in May 1932 and the signal box, installed in 1894, was replaced by a ground frame with tablet on 3rd July 1927. Then from 21st August 1930, the branch was worked by one token and effectively was 'one engine in steam'

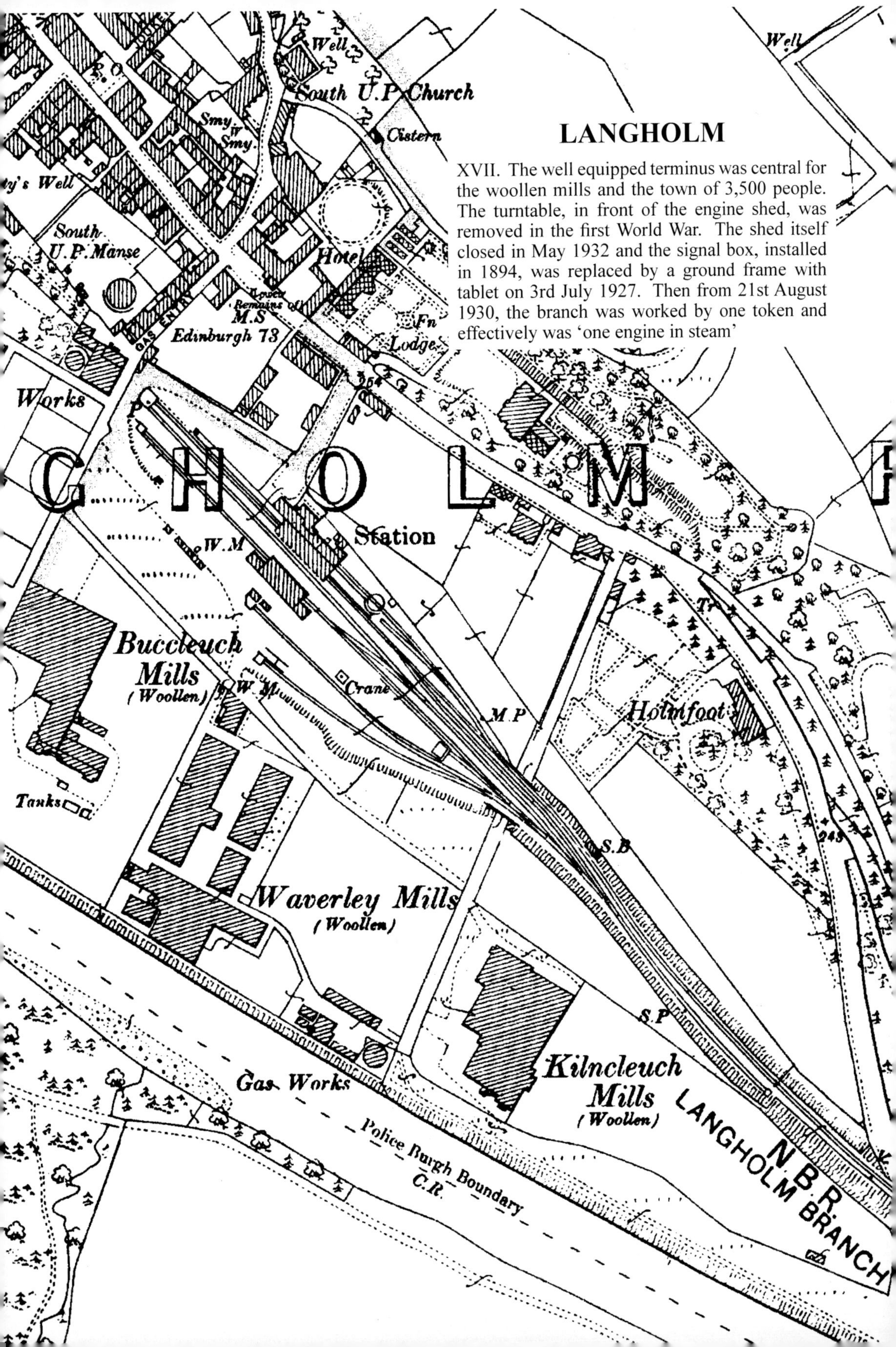

54. Here is NBR class R (J82) 0-6-0T no.22 *Langholm* at Langholm station in 1910 with crew and station staff. Built by Dugald Drummond in 1878, no.22 was based at Carlisle until its withdrawal in November 1925. It was out-stationed at Langholm but in April 1914, when the horse dandy was replaced on the Port Carlisle branch, no.22 was the first locomotive there. (R.W.Lynn coll.)

55. The relationship of the engine shed, water tower and station buildings is clearer in this photograph. Arriving trains had to be propelled out of the platform to enable the locomotive to run around the carriages before pushing them back under the station platform awning. (Stations UK)

56. *Protector* was the regular steam railcar at Langholm, though *Nettle* was also used. This photograph was taken in March 1939. *Protector* entered service in 1929, came to Carlisle in 1931 and remained there until withdrawn in June 1944. In 1932 it was rostered to make four round trips from Carlisle to Langholm between 9.30am and 10.01pm. (Real Photographs/R.W.Lynn coll.)

57. A class J39 0-6-0 was taking on water on 9th July 1949. The station had lost its awning, probably during World War II. The engine shed was still standing and goods services lasted until 17th September 1967. (R.W.Lynn coll.)

58. This was the road approach to the station taken on 3rd September 1955. In 1894, the locomotive shed was shortened to allow a general waiting room to be built and a new booking office to be provided. The platform was also lengthened. However, by 1964 only 350 passengers were using the 32 trains per week. (B.Connell/Photos of the Fifties)

59. This is a view from the town end of the platform with the branch train in the platform. The date is 30th June 1956. Creeper has beautified the wall of the goods shed which was equipped with a 4-ton crane. Two porters' barrows are ready waiting for parcels traffic. (N.E.Stead coll.)

60. While class J39 0-6-0 were standard locomotives on the branch in early British Railway days, 4MT 2-6-0 no.43139 was a regular performer in the latter years. In 1963 the water tank behind the roofless engine shed still had the 'bothy' underneath it. In earlier years this had a steam boiler in it to heat the foot warmers for first class passengers. (N.E.Stead coll.)

61. Our final photograph of the Langholm branch is of class 4MT 2-6-0 no.43028 shunting one of the three times weekly freight trains by the Waverley Mill at Langholm. We now return to the main line and the station north of Riddings Junction. (R.B.McCartney)

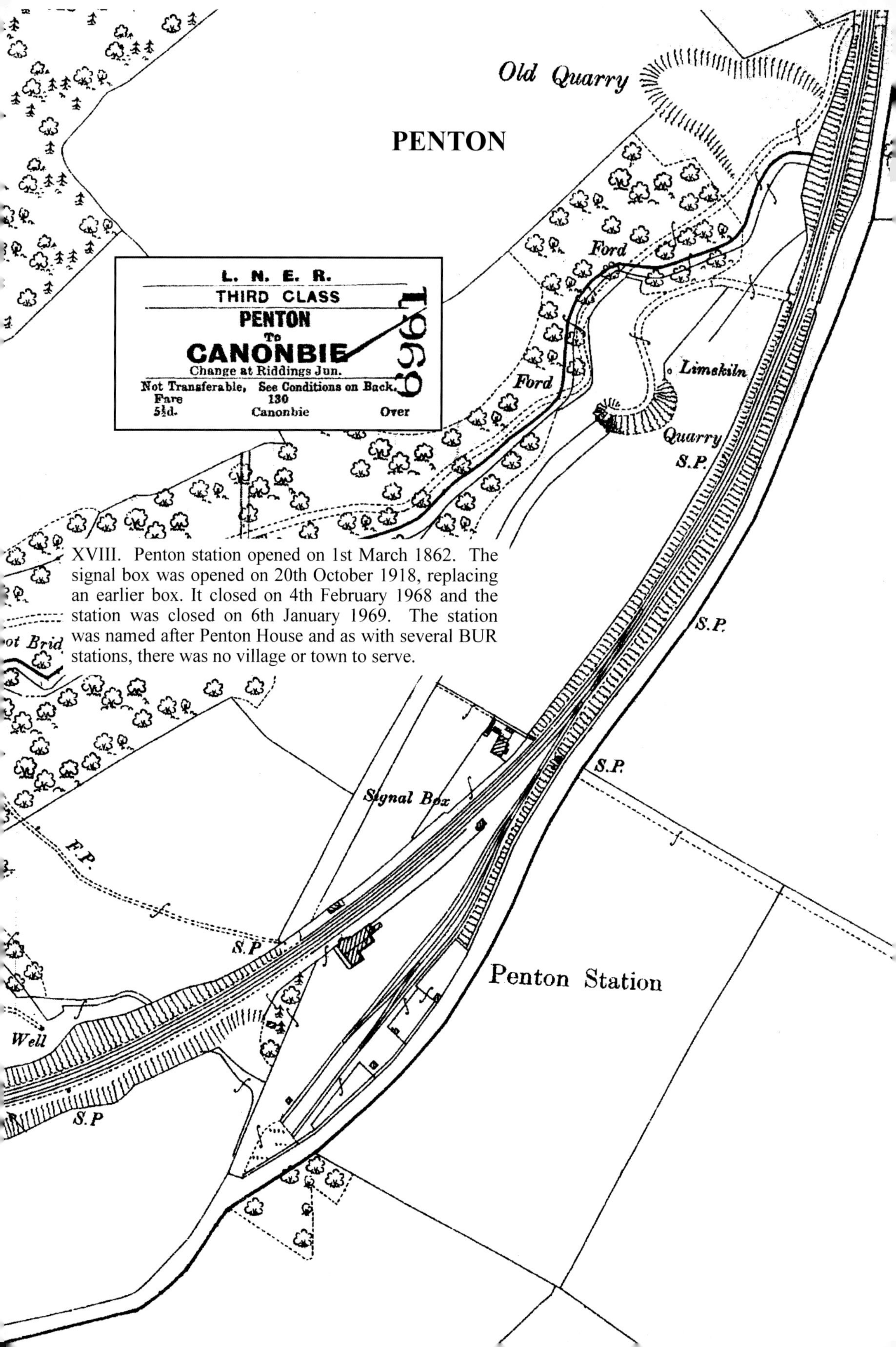

L. N. E. R.
THIRD CLASS
PENTON
To
CANONBIE
Change at Riddings Jun.
Not Transferable, See Conditions on Back.
Fare 130
5½d. Canonbie Over
1969

XVIII. Penton station opened on 1st March 1862. The signal box was opened on 20th October 1918, replacing an earlier box. It closed on 4th February 1968 and the station was closed on 6th January 1969. The station was named after Penton House and as with several BUR stations, there was no village or town to serve.

62. Class K3 2-6-0 no.61858 leaves with the 12.25pm Saturdays only Hawick to Carlisle stopping train on 26th May 1956. (The stationmaster's uniform trousers are hanging on the washing line!) (R.Leslie)

63. The station shows similarity in architecture to Lyneside. The railway was crossed by a wooden barrow way with neat wooden tracks to help the barrow to be hauled up the gravel platform ramp. An Edinburgh to Carlisle stopping train hauled by a Type 2 Bo-BoDE is being met by the stationmaster. (Stations UK)

64. Looking north this is a better view of the signal box and the down platform shelter. In early days there was a coal siding at the south end of the station and in the 1890s there was a private siding for Kingfield House to the north of the station. The goods yard was behind the main station building and closed on 9th October 1967. (R.W.Lynn)

65. Class B16/3 4-6-0 no.61439 was a rare visitor to the Waverley Route. It is climbing north of Penton on a class H through freight, close to the site of a quarry, lime and coal depot at Whatleyhirst. (L.N.Owen/N.E.Stead)

NOOK PASTURE

XIX. It opened on 2nd January 1864 without any station buildings or freight facilities. It appeared in the early timetables as one Saturday train, the up 07.57 from Kershopefoot, but had disappeared from the timetables by 1st January 1874. John Forster was a substantial shareholder of the BUR. His family owned Nook and Old Hall Farm and further east, Brownknowe Farm. Near Hirsthead is Pasture Well. From that, Pasture Beck runs to the railway which is level near the Carl Pool, between Milepost 79 and 79¼. Bridges 239, 240 and 241 and a major culvert are all more ornate than usual and all bordered Forster land. The station probably closed when John Forster ceased to be a major shareholder. This map is 6 ins to 1 mile.

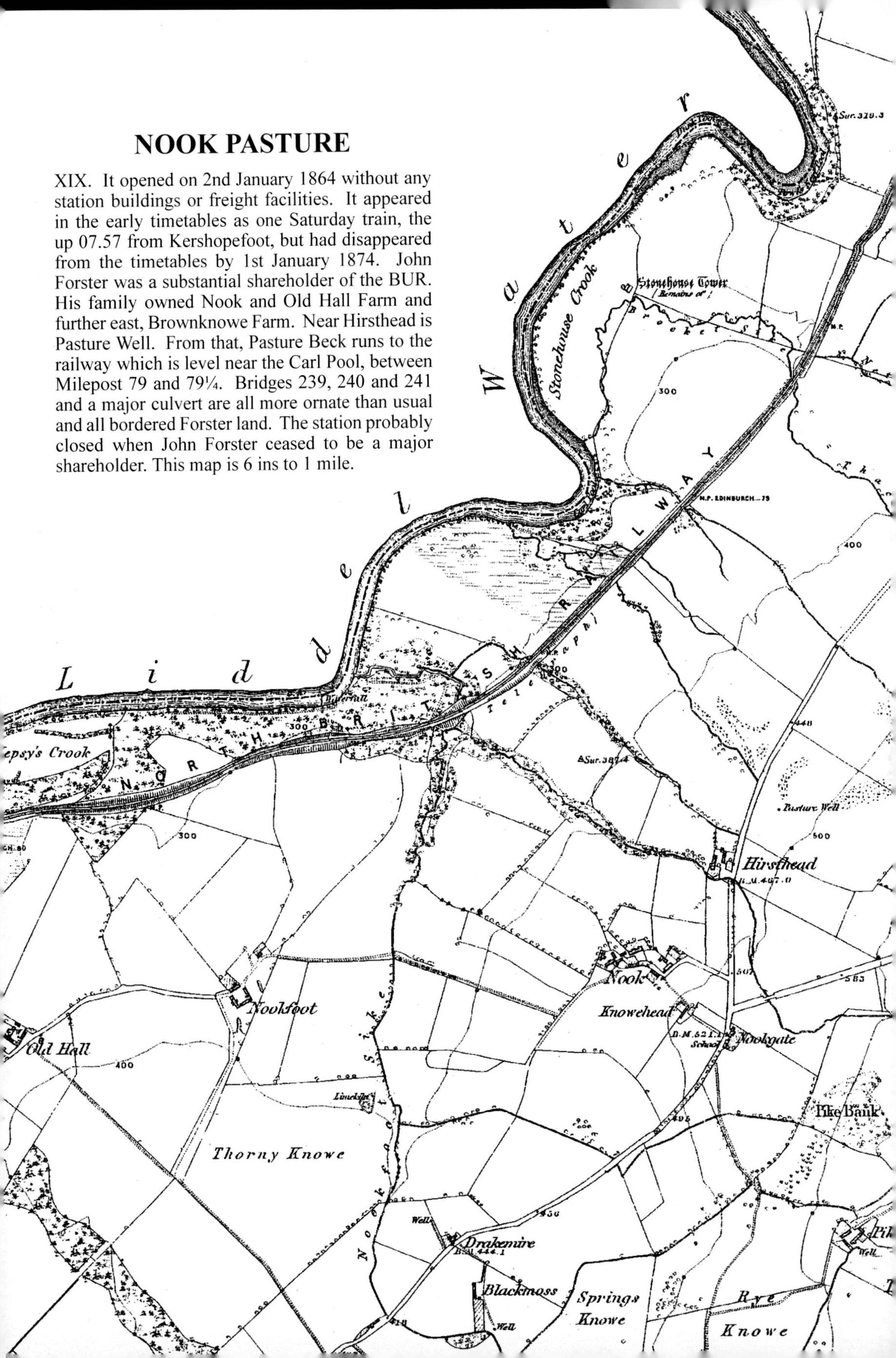

KERSHOPEFOOT

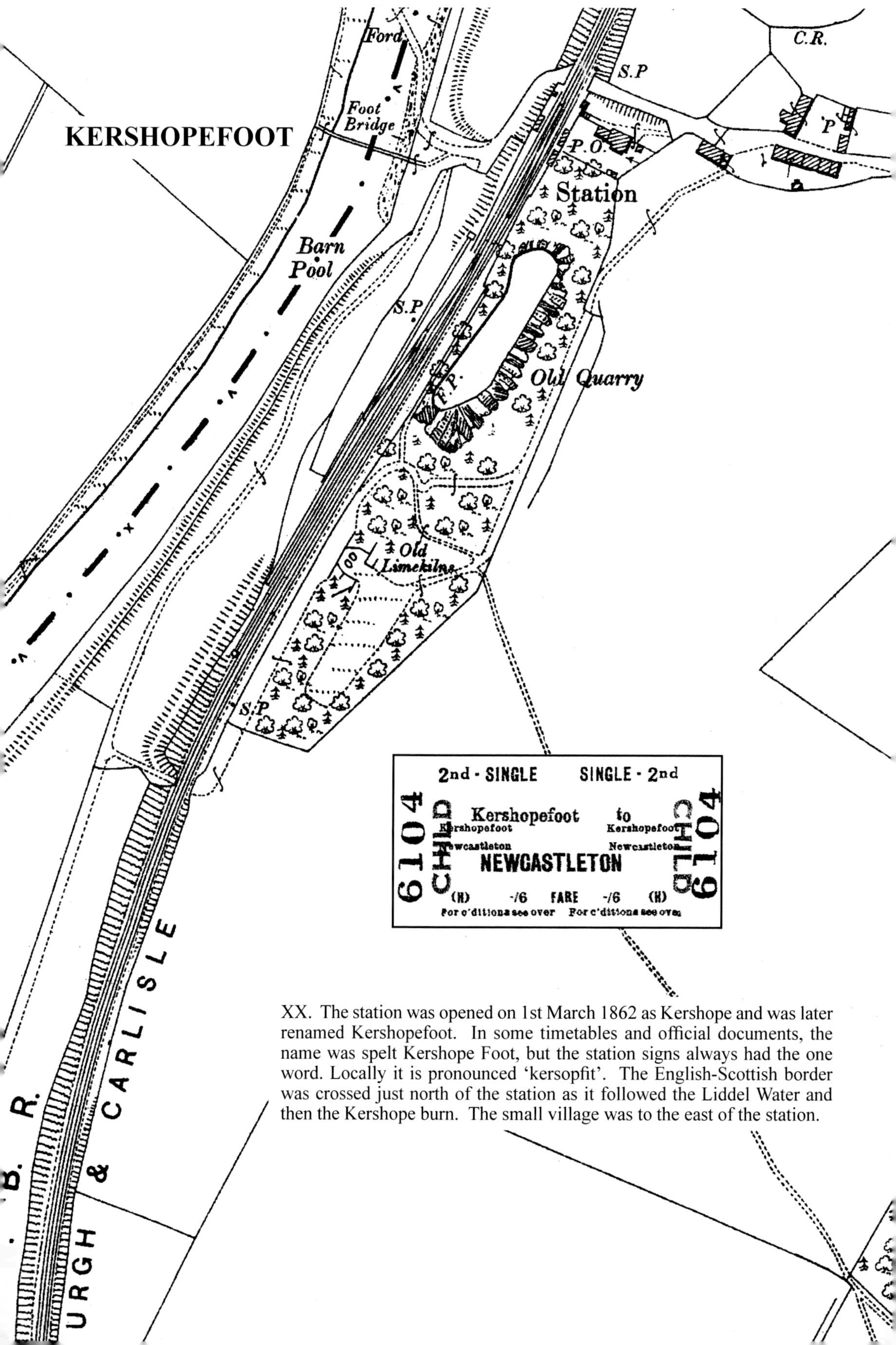

XX. The station was opened on 1st March 1862 as Kershope and was later renamed Kershopefoot. In some timetables and official documents, the name was spelt Kershope Foot, but the station signs always had the one word. Locally it is pronounced 'kersopfit'. The English-Scottish border was crossed just north of the station as it followed the Liddel Water and then the Kershope burn. The small village was to the east of the station.

66. This is an early postcard of Kershopefoot with a southbound freight train passing through the station. Before the bridge over the Liddel Water was built, there was no level crossing and access to the west bank was via a ford and an underpass under the platforms. The original signal box was on the up platform. The locomotive appears to be a Wheatley NBR class E 0-6-0 (LNER class J31). (R.B.McCartney coll.)

67. This is a clearer view of the station and its platforms. Visible from the railway was the Kershopefoot G.I.C. camp used for internees in World War I. In the Depression it was a training camp for the long term unemployed. Finally it was the base camp for Canadian lumberjacks of the Newfoundland Overseas Forestry Unit in World War II. (Lens of Sutton coll.)

68. The second signal box was opened on the down side on 5th March 1915 and closed 6th January 1969. The signalman is giving instructions to the crew of class 5MT 4-6-0 no.44886 fitted with a snowplough. The station was closed to goods on 28th December 1964 and was unstaffed from 27th March 1967. (N.Forrest/GNSRA/Transport Treasury)

LONDON AND NORTH EASTERN RAILWAY.

No. 696

—o—

..............................DEPARTMENT.

..............................STATION.

Date,..............................19

—o—

COUNTERPART.

—o—

CHURCH TRAIN FREE TICKET.

I hereby certify that.............................., *to whom*
(Name of Servant)
this Voucher is granted is a..............................*in the*
(Designation)
employment of the Company, and is entitled under the regulations printed hereon to..............................*Third Class Free*
(Name, in Writing)
Return Ticket, for use by the Church Train on Sunday, the
..............................19..............

Signature,..............................

The Servant in whose favour the Certificate is given must sign, in the space provided, for the number of Tickets actually issued to him in exchange for the Voucher.

Prog. No. of Tickets issued,..............................

Date issued,..............................

....

To .... STATION AGENT.

....

....

NOT TRANSFERABLE.

Est. 2871—3 Bks., 100 lvs.—2/33 ✠ (1956)

LONDON AND NORTH EASTERN RAILWAY
(SOUTHERN SCOTTISH AREA).

No. 696

CHURCH TRAIN FREE TICKET VOUCHER.

This Voucher, with the Certificate filled up and signed by the Station Agent or Locomotive or Permanent Way Department Foreman, in whose Pay-Bill the Servant to whom it is granted appears, must be exchanged at the Booking-Office for the Free Ticket or Tickets authorised.

A Church Train Free Ticket is available only between the issuing Station and Hawick or Newcastleton by the Sunday Church Train when run.

CERTIFICATE.

..............................DEPARTMENT,..............................STATION,

Date,..............................19

I hereby certify that.............................., *to whom*
(Name of Servant)
this Voucher is granted is a..............................*in the*
(Designation)
employment of the Company, and is entitled under the regulations printed hereon to..............................*Third Class Free Return Ticket, for use by the*
(Number, in Writing)
Church Train on Sunday, the..............................19..........

Signature,..............................

Will not be accepted if altered, unless the alteration is initialled by the Station Agent or Foreman.

The Servant in whose favour the Certificate is given must sign, in the space provided, for the number of Tickets actually issued to him in exchange for the Voucher.

Received in exchange for this Voucher..............................*Church Train Free Tickets.*

Signature..............................

PARTICULARS TO BE FILLED UP AT BOOKING-OFFICE.

Prog. No. on Tickets issued.............................. *Date issued,*..............................

..............................*Station Agent.*

Church Train Free Tickets must not be issued to, or used by, any other persons than the Company's Servants, the Wives and Children of such Servants residing with their Husbands or Parents (such children being dependent upon their parents), or other permanent members of the households of, and dependent upon such Servants of the Company: the Tickets are available for use only by the persons in whose favour they are given, and should any Voucher or Ticket be transferred or any improper use made thereof, the Servant to whom the Voucher is granted will be liable to instant dismissal, and the person abusing the privilege may be prosecuted for fraud.

NEWCASTLETON

XXI. Newcastleton was the only centre of population between Longtown and Hawick and even today its population is only 800. The station was central to the village and was well equipped for goods traffic. It is to the west of the Border forests. In World War II two Hunslet 2′ 0″ gauge diesel locomotives were delivered to the Forestry Commission for light railway use in the area.

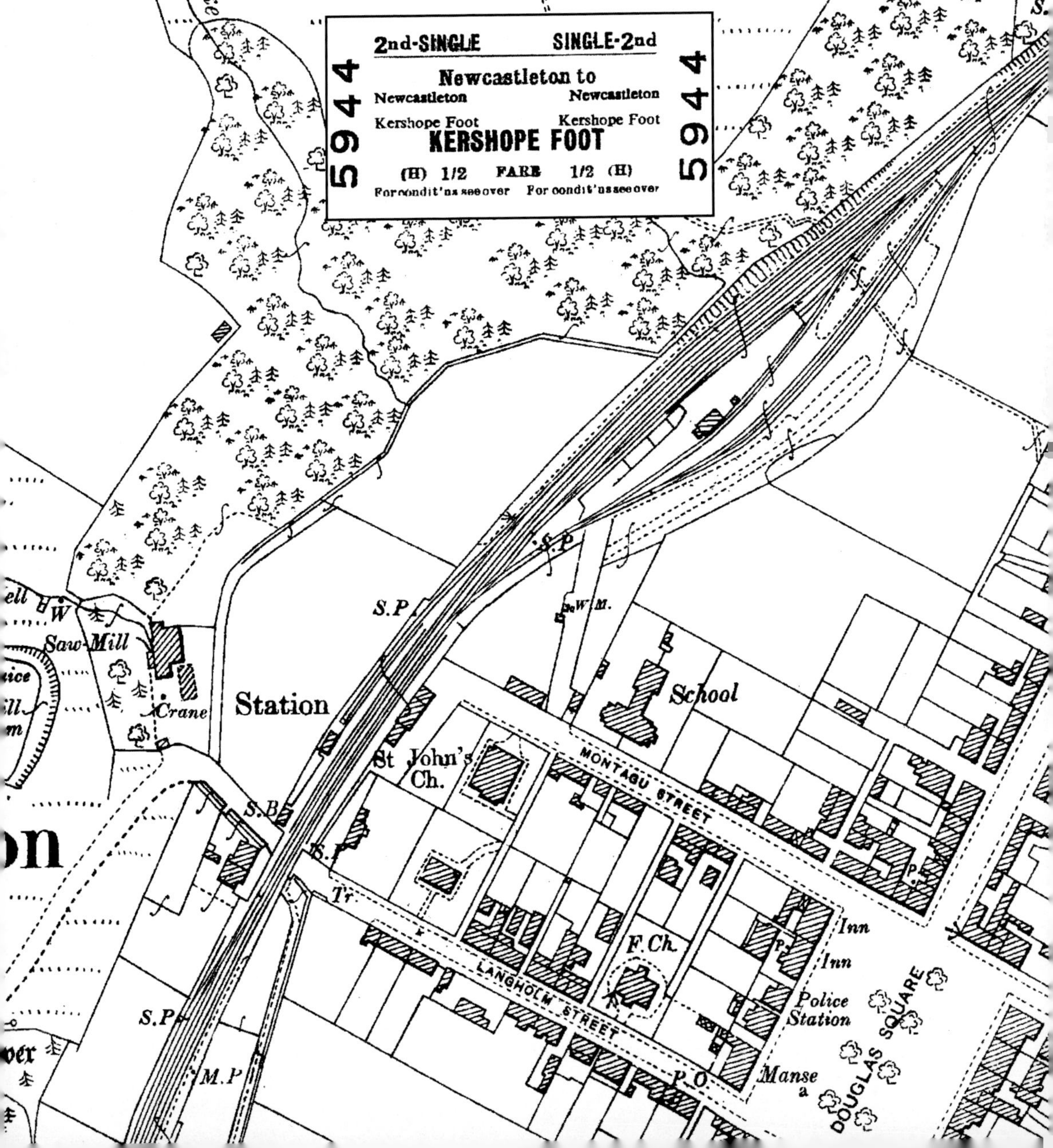

69. The station and the town look neat and tidy for this early 1900s postcard. To the east of the station in its own gardens is the Temperance Hotel. The station opened 1st March 1862 and closed 6th January 1969. The goods service had closed on 9th October 1967 and the land is now used as a caravan park. (R.W.Lynn coll.)

70. A closer view of the station buildings shows the good yards to the north. The floral efforts of the station staff are in evidence, as a banking locomotive, probably a class J31 0-6-0, backs into the station on the down line. (K.H.C.Taylor/R.W.Lynn coll.)

71. The Shires have always had a long association with the army and this shows the departure of a Volunteers train from Newcastleton to Hawick in World War I. It is a sad thought that many on the train would not have returned. (R.W.Lynn coll.)

72. Newcastleton is known locally as Copshawholm. This view of the station is to the south. It was taken on 25th June 1955 and is one of a series of photographs taken from this spot that can be roughly dated by the height of the trees in the plantation. (A.G.Ellis/R.W.Lynn coll.)

73. The goods yard to the north of the station was quite extensive and had a 2-ton crane. It was used for timber traffic from the Newcastleton Forest right up to closure. There was a proposal in 1999 to reopen Longtown to Whitrope as a way of removing timber from the much larger Kielder Forest. So far this has not materialised. (N.Forrest/GNSRA/Transport Treasury)

74. North of Newcastleton is the four arch viaduct at Sandholm over Hermitage Water. A Type 2 Bo-BoDE is hauling a down train towards Hawick. (N.Forrest/GNSRA/Transport Treasury)

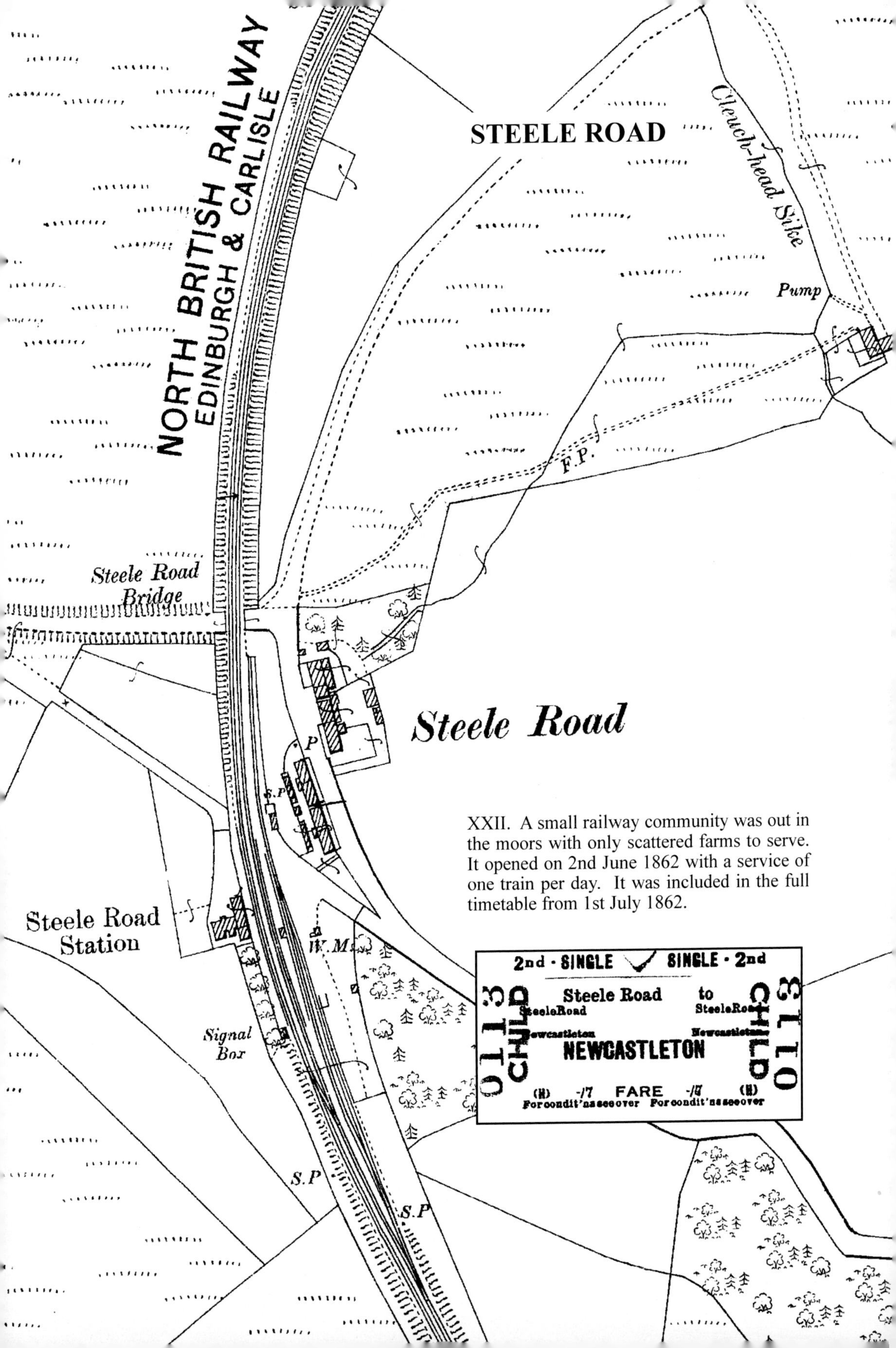

XXII. A small railway community was out in the moors with only scattered farms to serve. It opened on 2nd June 1862 with a service of one train per day. It was included in the full timetable from 1st July 1862.

75. The most famous train on the route was 'The Waverley' (London St Pancras-Edinburgh), hauled on 16th May 1959 by class A3 4-6-2 no.60037 *Hyperion*. It is approaching Steele Road from the south with the yard sidings diverging from the up line. (P.J.Robinson)

76. This 1906 view of the station buildings included staff and passengers. The buildings are on the down side and the photograph appears to have been taken from the goods yard with the fence the rear limit of the up platform. Goods services closed on 28th December 1964 and it was unstaffed from 27th March 1967. (R.W.Lynn coll.)

77. This view looking south shows the up platform and the fence more clearly. It also shows the signal box. The original box was destroyed by fire on 27th May 1914 to be replaced by this one on 8th September 1914. It was closed on 21st January 1965. (Lens of Sutton)

78. An English Electric Type 4 1-Co-Co-1 (Class 40) with its train to Hawick and beyond has stopped in the station. The local Bristol single deck bus is awaiting potential passengers for Bellingham via Kielder. This service replaced the Border Counties line closed in 1956. The hill behind rises to 1330 feet. (N.Forrest/GNSRA/Transport Treasury)

79. Class B1 4-6-0 no.61099 is leaving Steele Road with the 6.13pm Carlisle to Hawick stopping train in 1964. Steele Road bridge is by the first carriage. The photographer is standing on 'The Steele', the southern flank of Arnton Fell. (P.J.Robinson)

80. The severe winter of January 1963 was hard on the line and the rural communities it passed through. Class 4MT 0-6-0 no.44081 is leading the two class 5MT 4-6-0s on the snowplough team. While awaiting instructions at Steele Road box, the crews have time to pose for the camera. Note the very heavy tarpaulins between cabs and tenders. (P.Brock/R.W.Lynn coll.)

81. Break over, the snowploughs continue up the line towards Riccarton Junction. With a plough at each end, the three locomotives are battling with the drifts. (P.Brock/R.W.Lynn coll.)

82. The same location under Spring conditions and a long freight train is battling up the grade to Riccarton Junction with class K3 2-6-0 no.61936 leading and class D30 4-4-0 no. 62420 *Dominie Sampson* acting as banker. The date is 31st May 1952. (J.L.Stephenson/R.W.Lynn coll.)

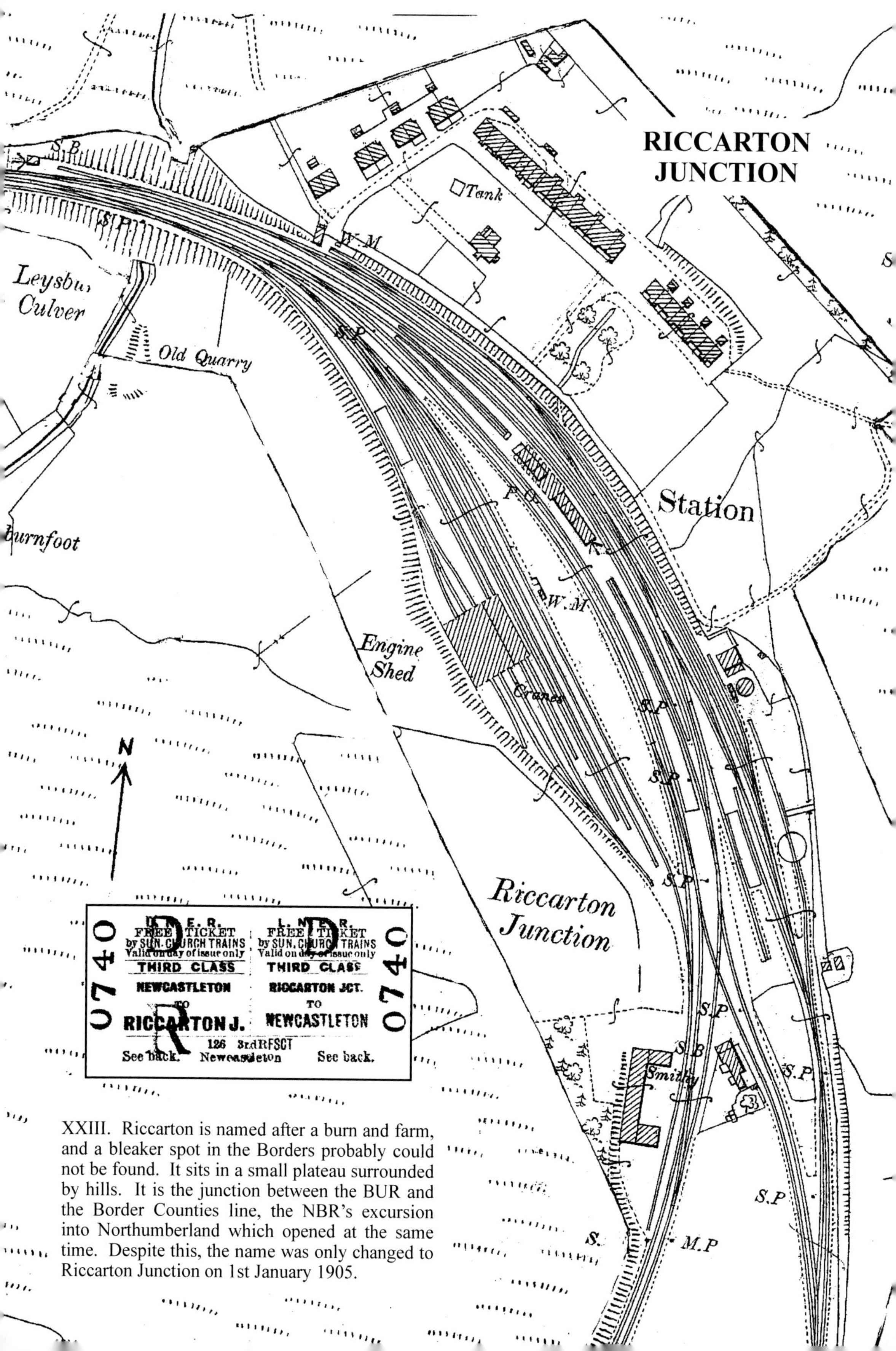

L. N. E. R.	L. N. E. R.
FREE TICKET	FREE TICKET
by SUN. CHURCH TRAINS	by SUN. CHURCH TRAINS
Valid on day of issue only	Valid on day of issue only
THIRD CLASS	THIRD CLASS
NEWCASTLETON	RICCARTON JCT.
TO	TO
RICCARTON J.	NEWCASTLETON
See back.	See back.

0740 · 0740 · 126 3rdRFSCT · Newcastleton

XXIII. Riccarton is named after a burn and farm, and a bleaker spot in the Borders probably could not be found. It sits in a small plateau surrounded by hills. It is the junction between the BUR and the Border Counties line, the NBR's excursion into Northumberland which opened at the same time. Despite this, the name was only changed to Riccarton Junction on 1st January 1905.

83. This early photograph from the north of the station shows the shed and works that were the reason for the construction of the railway village. The locomotive is probably a 0-4-2 on a train from the BCR. The workshops were moved in 1921 to Lochpark Engineering Sidings just south of Hawick and the village never recovered. (R.W.Lynn coll.)

84. The original engine shed was burnt down in 1900. Locomotives then stood in the open where the shed had been. On 4th August 1935 class J36 0-6-0 nos.9679 and 9692 and class D31 4-4-0 no.9640 are over the inspection pits. No.9640 was a stranger to Riccarton being normally a Dunfermline engine. (W.A.Camwell/R.W.Lynn coll.)

85. At 55ft the turntable was the largest between Carlisle and Edinburgh. There were two coaling stages in earlier days. The southern one was extended to provide an engine shed in 1945. The Border Counties line curves along the hillside while the BUR heads down the valley by Riccarton South signal box, which opened in 1881. The photograph's date is 3rd September 1955. (B.Connell/Photos of the Fifties)

86. Class J36 0-6-0 no.65232 is on shed with a 'Scott' class D30 4-4-0 behind it. The shed was closed in October 1958. Some of the sidings at Riccarton were used for storing wagons and locomotives over the years, including unusually, Great Northern Railway class D1 4-4-0 no.2214, one of several transferred north in 1925. (N.E.Stead coll.)

87. This 1912 postcard shows the station, platforms and the village terraces up on the hill. A local passenger train is in the bay platform. In the early years the village was terrorised by a gang of four wives. This problem was solved by transferring the employees and their wives to different areas of the country. (R.W.Lynn coll.)

88. The village housed 148 people in several streets of terraced houses with semi-detached and detached houses for the more senior staff and the stationmaster. There was no tarred road access to the village which was wholly rail served until the Border Counties line was lifted in 1958. (R.W.Lynn coll.)

89. This is the view of the station from the lowest terrace of the village. A class K3 2-6-0 is heading south with a class E express freight. Riccarton North signal box is in the centre distance. It opened in 1881, burned down and was rebuilt in the late 1940s, and closed on 15th April 1959. (E.E.Smith/R.W.Lynn coll.)

90. On the island platform was the telephone kiosk, sub post office and the village shop, the grocery branch of the Hawick Co-op Society. The refreshment room also served as the pub. A southbound passenger train is in the station. Outside the station is a freight train hauled by a class D49 4-4-0. The goods yard was closed on 6th February and the station became unstaffed from 27th March 1967. (M.Halbert/R.W.Lynn coll.)

91. The last full day of passenger service included this nine coach special hauled by Deltic class Co-CoDE no.9007 *Pinza*. The Friends of Riccarton Junction, formed in 1997, cleaned the derelict site and relaid a section of track in 2005. Following internal disputes, the scheme was abandoned in 2006 and the site handed back to the Forestry Commission. (G.W.Morrison)

92. Class V2 2-6-2 no.60824 heading north from Riccarton with a class D express fitted freight, is passing the closed Riccarton North signal box. On Saughtree Fell the hillside has been ploughed for afforestation. (P.J.Robinson)

WHITROPE

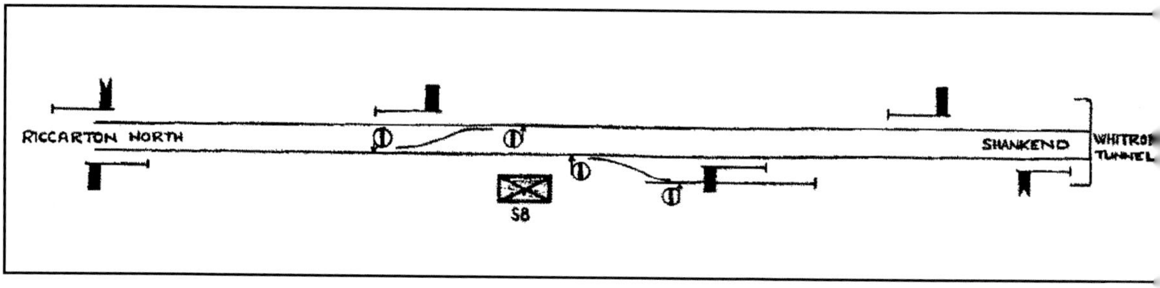

XXIV. Whitrope Siding was an unadvertised halt officially for railway staff only. The siding was used to stable bank pilots waiting to return to Hawick or Newcastleton. It was in the working timetables by 1st April 1914. This is the signalling diagram drawn by G.Hall, the signalman on the last day.

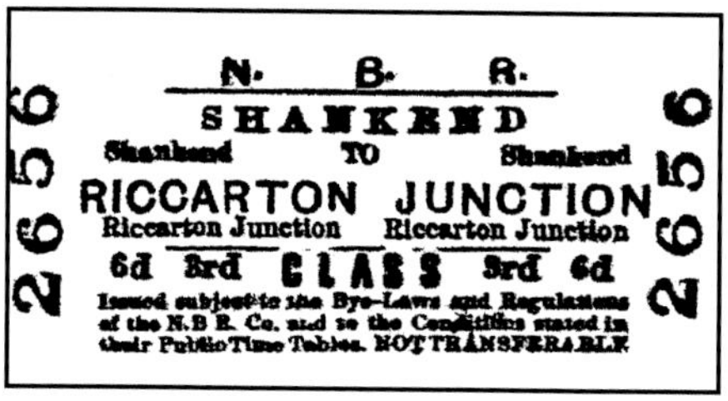

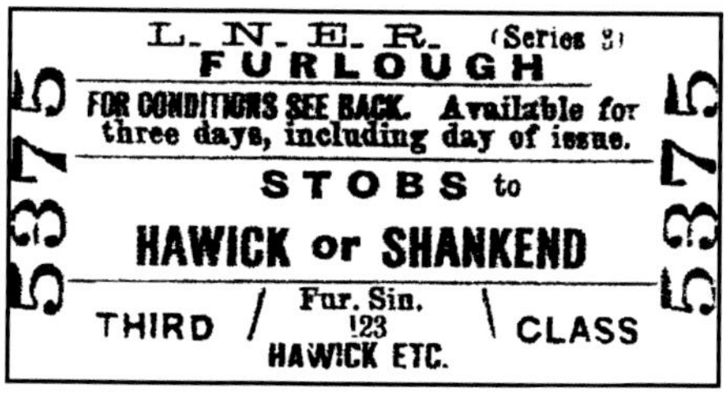

Readers of this book may be interested in the following societies:

Langholm Archive Group
c/o R.B.McCartney, Cairndhu, Walter Street, Langholm, DG13 0AX
www.langholmarchive.org

North British Railway Study Group
c/o R.W.Lynn, 2, Brecken Court, Saltwell Road South, Low Fell, Gateshead, NE9 6EY
www.nbrstudygroup.co.uk

Railway Correspondence and Travel Society, Scottish Branch
℅ E.Williams, Seacroft, Eglington Terrace, Skelmorlie, Ayrshire, PA17 5ER
www.rcts.org.uk

Waverley Route Heritage Association
Signal Box Cottage, Whitrope, Hawick, Roxburghshire, TD9 9TY
www.wrha.org.uk

93. The Whitrope Siding signal box and the siding itself were protected from drifting snow by a fence of old sleepers. The siding closed to the public on 24th February 1964 and the signal box closed on 6th November 1967. (Stations UK)

94. Whitrope Siding never had a platform. Access to and from trains was via the step ladder in the guard's brake van. It was never classified as a station until it was listed in the 1968 closure notice. Passengers are seen getting off a Carlisle bound train on 20th September 1952. (J.W.Armstrong Trust)

95. The scene is very white and bleak, as two Type 1 (class 17) Bo-BoDE pass Whitrope after closure in December 1969 with a track-dismantling train. D8586 and its twin were built by Clayton and used for freight on the line, usually in pairs with two crews, which made them rather uneconomic. (R.B.McCartney)

96. Just north of Whitrope siding was Whitrope summit and Whitrope tunnel. On 4th June 1960 class V2 2-6-2 no.60922 is approaching the tunnel mouth with a north bound passenger train. Once again a sleeper fence protects the cutting before the tunnel from drifting snow. (P.B.Booth/N.E.Stead coll.)

97. Another class V2 2-6-2 no.60835 is struggling out of the southern entrance of the tunnel with a class C perishable freight being banked in the rear. After the train has breasted the summit, the banker will come off at Whitrope Siding. (N.Forrest/GNSRA/Transport Treasury)

98. Whitrope siding was from 2001 the home of the Waverley Route Heritage Association. Whitrope is therefore the first 'station' to re-appear and the 21st century version boasts a two coach platform and even its own car park. The first locomotive to arrive at the site was 0-6-0DM J.Fowler's no.4240015 originally at Hartlepool Power Station. It came on site on 9th December 2009. (G.Ruderham/WRHA)

SHANKEND

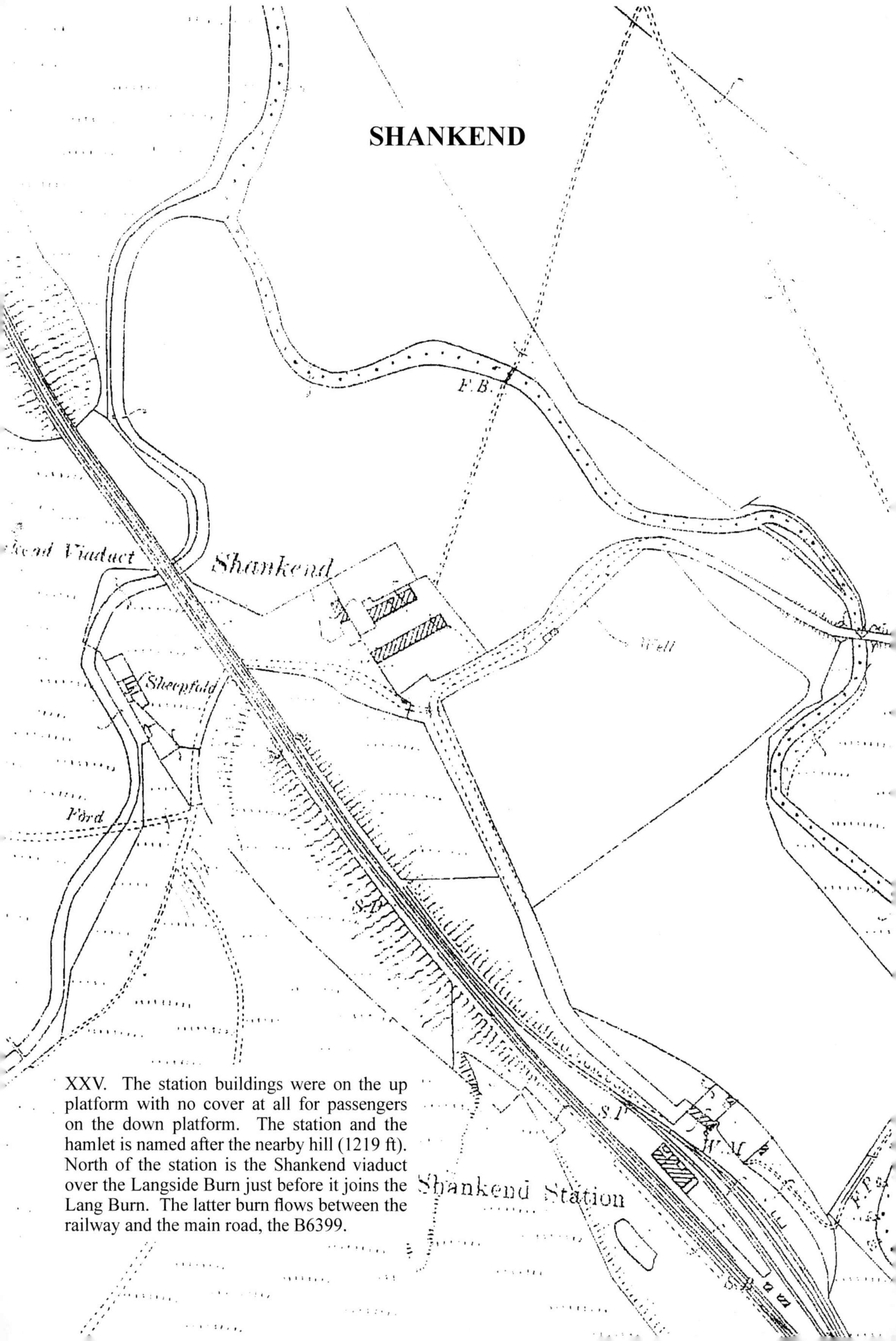

XXV. The station buildings were on the up platform with no cover at all for passengers on the down platform. The station and the hamlet is named after the nearby hill (1219 ft). North of the station is the Shankend viaduct over the Langside Burn just before it joins the Lang Burn. The latter burn flows between the railway and the main road, the B6399.

99. The station was photographed from an up train. The coaches are in the loop siding. The gardens in July 1952 are really magnificent considering the windswept location of the station. The lattice and ladder, which were another feature of the line, are part of the tall NBR signal. (R.W.Lynn coll.)

100. This view shows the buildings, the footbridge and the down platform. The first signal box was commissioned on 20th July 1888 and replaced by the present one on 24th January 1916. The station was unstaffed from 3rd July 1961 and closed to goods traffic on 28th December 1964. (R.W.Lynn coll.)

101. At the south end of the station were the sidings and from here the up banking locomotives were attached for the climb to Whitrope. Class V2 2-6-2 no.60937 is on an up freight with class J36 0-6-0 no.65316 and several goods guards vans in the sidings. The Reid 0-6-0 is fitted with a small snowplough but appears not to be preparing to bank, as the catch points are not yet locked out. (G.Hall/R.W.Lynn coll.)

102. An atmospheric picture of the southern end of the Shankend viaduct with a 2MT class 2-6-0 banking a freight from Hawick. The viaduct crosses the Langside Burn with 15 arches and is 597 yards long. (R.Barbour)

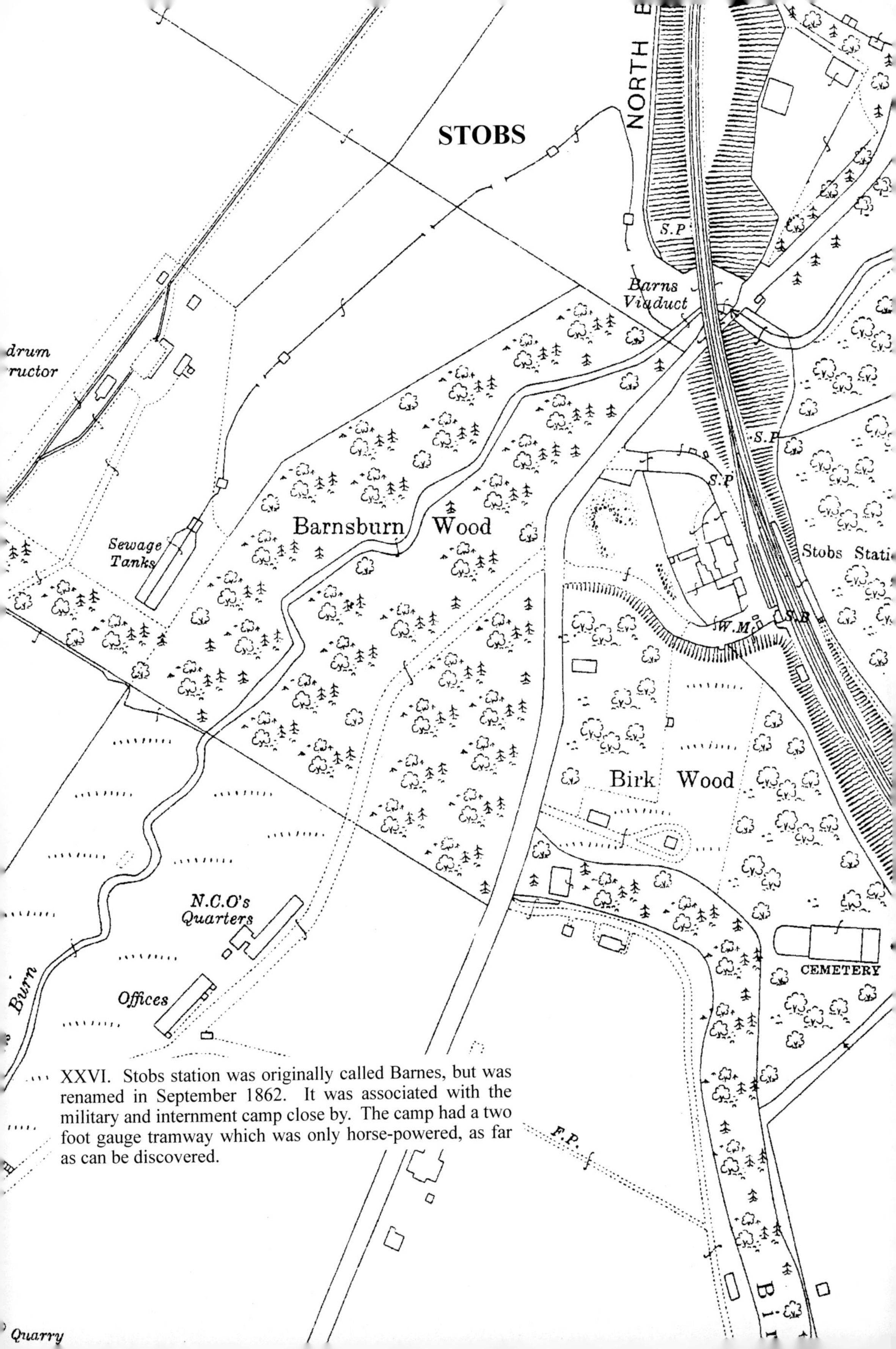

XXVI. Stobs station was originally called Barnes, but was renamed in September 1862. It was associated with the military and internment camp close by. The camp had a two foot gauge tramway which was only horse-powered, as far as can be discovered.

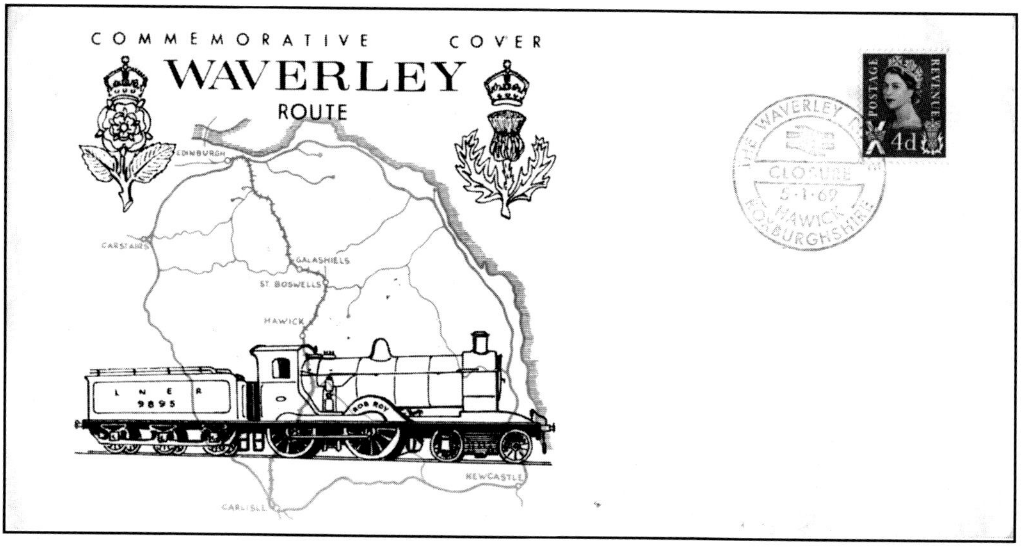

Last day cover.

103. A troop train is setting off for Hawick and beyond during World War I. There are ladies on the platform to see them off and the heavy baggage has come in the horse drawn military transport. (R.B.McCartney coll.)

104. This is still looking north with the white fence under the footbridge and the short siding full of horseboxes and vans. The station became unstaffed and the goods yard closed on 3rd July 1961. The signal box was opened on 20th July 1888 and closed on 23rd December 1962. The station closed on the same day as the whole line. (R.W.Lynn coll.)

105. The cropped picture includes the station buildings as class 5MT 4-6-0 no.44767 heads through with an unusual freight train comprising three Hunslet class 05 0-6-0DM going north to a scrapyard. D2593/5/7, D2608/17 made this journey and these are three from that number. No.44767 has Stephenson link motion and has been preserved, as *Stephenson*, in Northumberland. (R.B.McCartney)

STOBS CAMP

XXVII. Stobs camp was bought by the War Office in 1903 from Elliot of Stobs Castle as a training ground. It was served by a set of sidings that could take up to four trains. There was an interchange platform connected with the tramway which was sometimes referred to as a private station. This sketch map, at 4 ½ inches to 1 mile, shows the sidings, the camp and the military tramway.

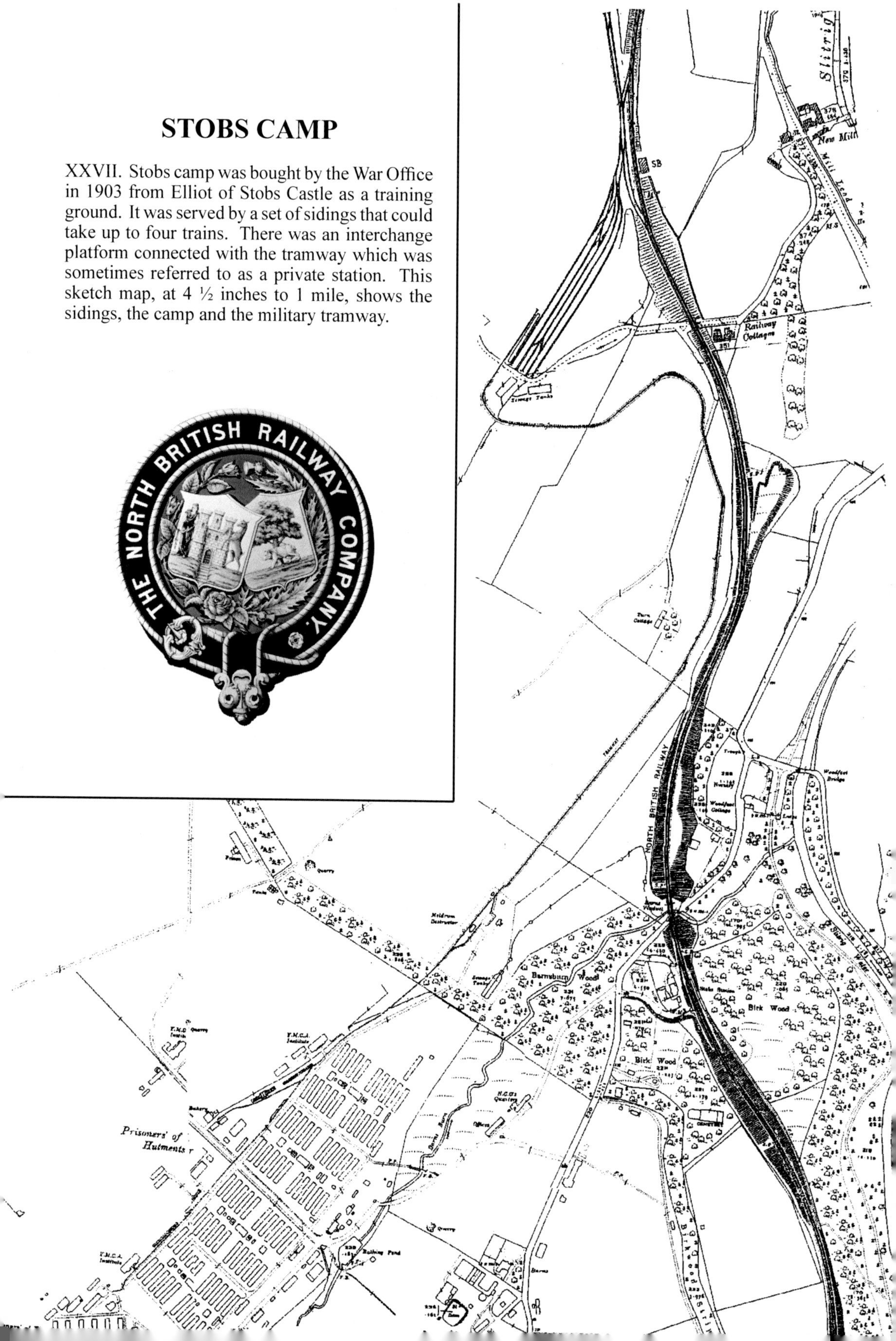

106. Stobs Camp could initially take 5,000 soldiers. In the 1914-1918 war it was opened for the internment of civilians. These were then sent to the Isle of Man and prisoners of war replaced them. When POW labour was made available, the camp became the main administration centre in Scotland. By 1915, 15,000 people were billeted on the site. (R.W.Lynn coll.)

A diagram for Stobs Camp signal box showing the original layout and the simplified structure from 1928. (R.B.McCartney coll.)

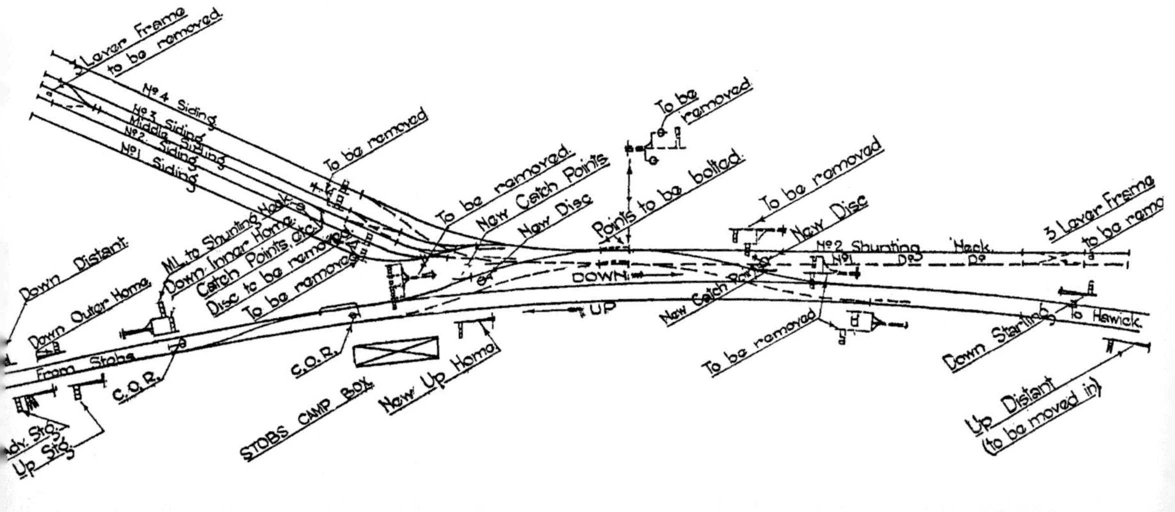

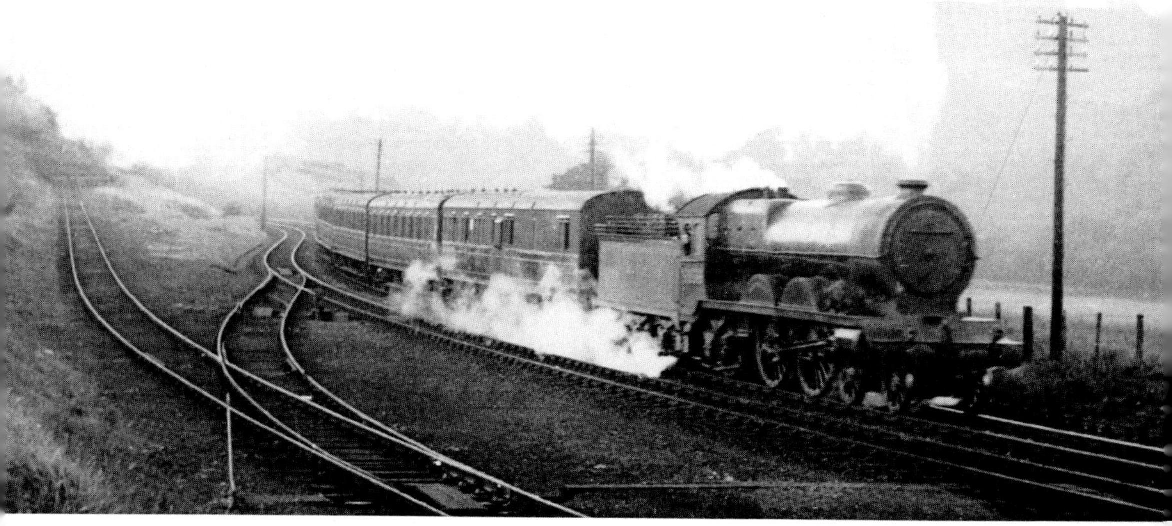

107. A class C11 4-4-2 is taking a Sunday excursion to Silloth in 1931 and is passing the head-shunt for the camp sidings. Extended in World War II, the camp then became a resettlement centre for 2,000 Polish soldiers. It was kept as a summer camp after 1947, but became derelict and was sold off in 1959. (R.B.Hadden/R.W.Lynn coll.)

108. Stobs Camp box was the biggest signal box on the line with 85 levers and worked by two men on three shifts. The military specials were added as 'notices' in the working timetables. In the 1950s, there were several specials bringing 'Z' reservists in and out at fortnightly intervals mainly from Glasgow and the north. (R.W.Lynn coll.)

109. This shows the network of sidings at Stobs Camp box. The camp tents are on the distant hillside. The sidings were controlled by these tall and distinctive signal lattices. (R.W.Lynn coll.)

110. This rather poor photograph shows at least three troop trains. A very long train on the up line is distantly by the Stobs Camp box, class K (D34) 4-4-0 no.9502, *Glen Fintaig*, is on the head-shunt and 'Intermediate' class M (D32) 4-4-0 no.890 on a train of horseboxes for a cavalry unit. (R.W.Lynn coll.)

HAWICK

XXVIII. The first station in Hawick was opened on 29th October 1849 and was served by the line from Edinburgh via Galashiels. When the second station was opened on 1st July 1862, the first became the goods station on the same day. The first station was a terminus but the new through station curved south and straddled the River Teviot on a high bridge. A population of 18,500 in 1901 had decreased by 2,000 by 1961 and has continued to decrease since then.

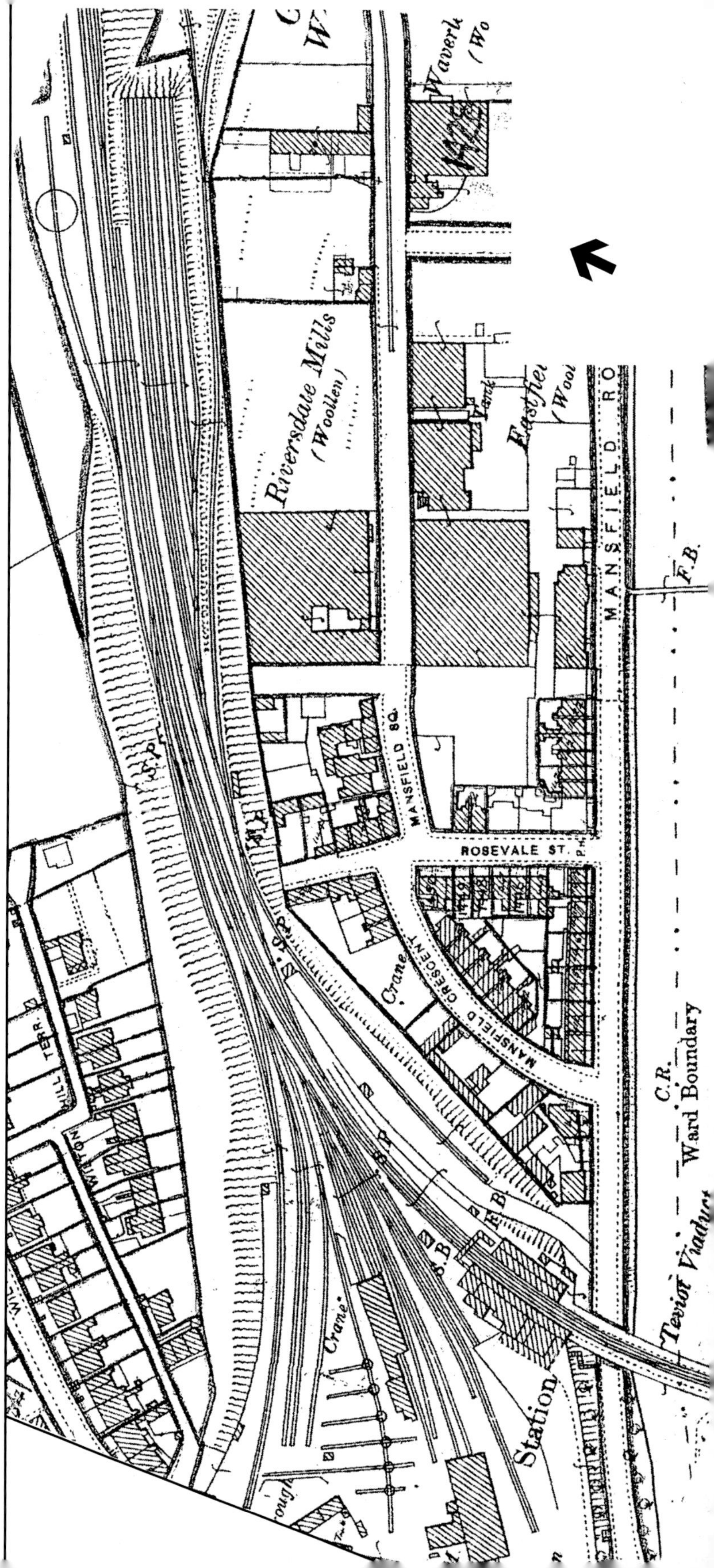

111. This is the station approach from the road taken about 1910. The stationmaster's accommodation was the upper storey of the station. An elementary timber yard is in the goods yard and the goods shed was off left. The goods yard closed on 28th April 1969. The signal box was raised in 1913 to improve the visibility. (R.W.Lynn coll.)

112. The very popular vantage point was at the end of Wilton Hill Terrace and this is the station in the 1950s. The goods yard is behind the plume of steam coming from the class J36 0-6-0 no.65331 in the shed yard. There is also another class J36 and a 2MT 2-6-0 no.78046. Behind the tall signal box is the dominating parcels hoist used by porters and Post Office staff. (Hawick News/R.W.Lynn coll.)

113. Class D34 4-4-0 no. 62490 *Glen Fintaig* is waiting to depart with an up stopping train for Carlisle. There was a push button in Hawick South signal box that rang a bell in the Station Hotel alerting customers when a train was shortly to depart. Where the platforms extended on to the Teviot viaduct, they were surfaced with wooden planks. (N.E.Stead coll.)

114. There was a short siding behind the north end of the up platform and the banking locomotive often waited there for the next southbound train that expected a push. The banking duties were identified by head codes. Here class J36 0-6-0 no.65317 is ready for duty 245 on 6th September 1955. (R.R.Darsley)

115. Local services were run by diesel multiple units from 1966. On 5th January 1969, the last day of operation, a class 101 has brought the 11.25am from Edinburgh to Hawick. The station was well equipped but most of the facilities were on the down platform. The depth of our researches is such that we know the dog was called Mickey! (R.B.McCartney)

116. The up platform buildings are more clearly shown, as the crowd gather to protest at the closure of the line. Note the coffin on the station barrow. The Hawick pilot, a Clayton Type 1, which was sent ahead of the final train was stopped by more protesters at Newcastleton. Final demolition of all facilities at Hawick, including the Teviot viaduct, took place by 1975 and the site today is home to Teviotdale Leisure Centre. (K.A.Gray)

HAWICK SHED

117. Hawick and its sub-sheds had a total allocation of 30 locomotives in 1923. In this 1960s view of the shed yard there are class D30 4-4-0 no.62423 *Dugald Dalgetty* a class J35 0-6-0 and a K3 class 2-6-0 taking water. The fourth locomotive is a visitor from Parkhead, Glasgow, a class K2 2-6-0, no.61755. An up train is in the station. (R.W.Lynn coll.)

118. Here the shed is seen from the down platform north end. An all NBR line-up consists of class D30 4-4-0 no.62423, *Dugald Dalgetty*, class C15 4-4-2T no.67477 and a class J36 0-6-0 no.65232, with an old six-wheeled NBR coach in the back of the yard. (R.W.Lynn coll.)

119. The shed was opened on 1st November 1849. It was re-roofed in 1955. Class K3 2-6-0 no.61984 is in the foreground. Behind is the class J36 0-6-0 no.65331 with a tender cab. Many of Hawick's J36s had tender cabs because of the inclement weather. (E.E.Smith/R.W.Lynn coll.)

120. Standard locomotives arrived in Hawick Shed. Class 2MT 2-6-0 nos.78046/47 were introduced in 1953 and 78048/49 were transferred later from St Margaret's. The shed closed on 3rd January 1966 but remained a booking-on-point for train crews until the closure of the line. A sad time indeed. (S.Murdoch/GNSRA/Transport Treasury)

MP **Middleton Press**

EVOLVING THE ULTIMATE RAIL ENCYCLOPEDIA

Easebourne Lane, Midhurst, West Sussex.
GU29 9AZ Tel:01730 813169

www.middletonpress.co.uk email:info@middletonpress.co.uk
A-978 0 906520 B- 978 1 873793 C- 978 1 901706 D-978 1 904474
E - 978 1 906008 F - 978 1 908174

All titles listed below were in print at time of publication - please check current availability by looking at our website - ***www.middletonpress.co.uk*** or by requesting a Brochure which includes our *LATEST* RAILWAY TITLES also our TRAMWAY, TROLLEYBUS, MILITARY and COASTAL series

A
Abergavenny to Merthyr C 91 8
Abertillery & Ebbw Vale Lines D 84 5
Aberystwyth to Carmarthen E 90 1
Allhallows - Branch Line to A 62 8
Alton - Branch Lines to A 11 6
Andover to Southampton A 82 6
Ascot - Branch Lines around A 64 2
Ashburton - Branch Line to B 95 4
Ashford - Steam to Eurostar B 67 1
Ashford to Dover A 48 2
Austrian Narrow Gauge D 04 3
Avonmouth - BL around D 42 5
Aylesbury to Rugby D 91 3
B
Baker Street to Uxbridge D 90 6
Bala to Llandudno E 87 1
Banbury to Birmingham D 27 2
Banbury to Cheltenham E 63 5
Bangor to Holyhead F 01 7
Bangor to Portmadoc E 72 7
Barking to Southend C 80 2
Barmouth to Pwllheli E 53 6
Barry - Branch Lines around D 50 0
Bartlow - Branch Lines to F 27 7
Bath Green Park to Bristol C 36 9
Bath to Evercreech Junction A 60 4
Beamish 40 years on rails E94 9
Bedford to Wellingborough D 31 9
Birmingham to Wolverhampton E253
Bletchley to Cambridge D 94 4
Bletchley to Rugby E 07 9
Bodmin - Branch Lines around B 83 1
Bournemouth to Evercreech Jn A 46 8
Bournemouth to Weymouth A 57 4
Bradshaw's Guide 1866 F 05 5
Bradshaw's History F18 5
Bradshaw's Rail Times 1850 F 13 0
Bradshaw's Rail Times 1895 F 11 6
Branch Lines series - see town names
Brecon to Neath D 43 2
Brecon to Newport D 16 6
Brecon to Newtown E 06 2
Brighton to Eastbourne A 16 1
Brighton to Worthing A 03 1
Bristol to Taunton D 03 6
Bromley South to Rochester B 23 7
Bromsgrove to Birmingham D 87 6
Bromsgrove to Gloucester D 73 9
Broxbourne to Cambridge F16 1
Brunel - A railtour D 74 6
Bude - Branch Line to B 29 9
Burnham to Evercreech Jn B 68 0
C
Cambridge to Ely D 55 5
Canterbury - BLs around B 58 9
Cardiff to Dowlais (Cae Harris) E 47 5
Cardiff to Pontypridd E 95 6
Cardiff to Swansea E 42 0
Carlisle to Hawick E 85 7
Carmarthen to Fishguard E 66 6
Caterham & Tattenham Corner B251
Central & Southern Spain NG E 91 8
Chard and Yeovil - BLs a C 30 7
Charing Cross to Dartford A 75 8
Charing Cross to Orpington A 96 3
Cheddar - Branch Line to B 90 9
Cheltenham to Andover C 43 7
Cheltenham to Redditch D 81 4
Chester to Birkenhead F 21 5
Chester to Rhyl E 93 2
Chester to Warrington F 40 6
Chichester to Portsmouth A 14 7
Clacton and Walton - BLs to F 04 8
Clapham Jn to Beckenham Jn B 36 7
Cleobury Mortimer - BLs a E 18 5
Clevedon & Portishead - BLs to D180
Consett to South Shields E 57 4
Cornwall Narrow Gauge D 56 2
Corris and Vale of Rheidol E 65 9
Craven Arms to Llandeilo E 35 2
Craven Arms to Wellington E 33 8
Crawley to Littlehampton A 34 5
Cromer - Branch Lines around C 26 0
Croydon to East Grinstead B 48 0
Crystal Palace & Catford Loop B 87 1
Cyprus Narrow Gauge E 13 0
D
Darjeeling Revisited F 09 3
Darlington Leamside Newcastle E 28 4
Darlington to Newcastle D 98 2
Dartford to Sittingbourne B 34 3
Denbigh - Branch Lines around F 32 1
Derwent Valley - BL to the D 06 7
Devon Narrow Gauge E 09 3
Didcot to Banbury D 02 9
Didcot to Swindon C 84 0
Didcot to Winchester C 13 0
Dorset & Somerset NG D 76 0
Douglas - Laxey - Ramsey E 75 8
Douglas to Peel C 88 8
Douglas to Port Erin C 55 0
Douglas to Ramsey D 39 5
Dover to Ramsgate A 78 9
Dublin Northwards in 1950s E 31 4
Dunstable - Branch Lines to E 27 7
E
Ealing to Slough C 42 0
Eastbourne to Hastings A 27 7
East Cornwall Mineral Railways D 22 7
East Croydon to Three Bridges A 53 6
Eastern Spain Narrow Gauge E 56 7
East Grinstead - BLs to A 07 9
East London - Branch Lines of C 44 4
East London Line B 80 0
East of Norwich - Branch Lines E 69 7
Effingham Junction - BLs a A 74 1
Ely to Norwich C 90 1
Enfield Town & Palace Gates D 32 6
Epsom to Horsham A 30 7
Eritrean Narrow Gauge E 38 3
Euston to Harrow & Wealdstone C 89 5
Exeter to Barnstaple B 15 2
Exeter to Newton Abbot C 49 9
Exeter to Tavistock B 69 5
Exmouth - Branch Lines to B 00 8
F
Fairford - Branch Line to A 52 9
Falmouth, Helston & St. Ives C 74 1
Fareham to Salisbury A 67 3
Faversham to Dover B 05 3
Felixstowe & Aldeburgh - BL to D 20 3
Fenchurch Street to Barking C 20 8
Festiniog - 50 yrs of enterprise C 83 3
Festiniog 1946-55 E 01 7
Festiniog in the Fifties B 68 8
Festiniog in the Sixties B 91 6
Ffestiniog in Colour 1955-82 F 25 3
Finsbury Park to Alexandra Pal C 02 8
Frome to Bristol B 77 0
G
Gloucester to Bristol D 35 7
Gloucester to Cardiff D 66 1
Gosport - Branch Lines around A 36 9
Greece Narrow Gauge D 72 2
H
Hampshire Narrow Gauge D 36 4
Harrow to Watford D 14 2
Harwich & Hadleigh - BLs to F 02 4
Hastings to Ashford A 37 6
Hawick to Galashiels F 36 9
Hawkhurst - Branch Line to A 66 6
Hayling - Branch Line to A 12 3
Hay-on-Wye - BL around D 92 0
Haywards Heath to Seaford A 28 4
Hemel Hempstead - BLs to D 88 3
Henley, Windsor & Marlow - BLa C77 2
Hereford to Newport D 54 8
Hertford & Hatfield - BLs a E 58 1
Hertford Loop E 71 0
Hexham to Carlisle D 75 3
Hexham to Hawick F 08 6
Hitchin to Peterborough D 07 4
Holborn Viaduct to Lewisham A 81 9
Horsham - Branch Lines to A 02 4
Huntingdon - Branch Line to A 93 2
I
Ilford to Shenfield C 97 0
Ilfracombe - Branch Line to B 21 3
Industrial Rlys of the South East A 09 3
Ipswich to Saxmundham C 41 3
Isle of Wight Lines - 50 yrs C 12 3
Italy Narrow Gauge F 17 8
K
Kent Narrow Gauge C 45 1
Kidderminster to Shrewsbury E 10 9
Kingsbridge - Branch Line to C 98 7
Kings Cross to Potters Bar E 62 8
Kingston & Hounslow Loops A 83 3
Kingswear - Branch Line to C 17 8
L
Lambourn - Branch Line to C 70 3
Launceston & Princetown - BLs C 19 2
Lewisham to Dartford A 92 5
Lines around Wimbledon B 75 6
Liverpool Street to Chingford D 01 2
Liverpool Street to Ilford C 34 5
Llandeilo to Swansea E 46 8
London Bridge to Addiscombe B 20 6
London Bridge to East Croydon A 58 1
Longmoor - Branch Lines to A 41 3
Looe - Branch Line to C 22 2
Lowestoft - BLs around E 40 6
Ludlow to Hereford E 14 7
Lydney - Branch Lines around E 26 0
Lyme Regis - Branch Line to A 45 1
Lynton - Branch Line to B 04 6
M
Machynlleth to Barmouth E 54 3
Maesteg and Tondu Lines E 06 2
Majorca & Corsica Narrow Gauge F 41 3
March - Branch Lines around B 09 1
Marylebone to Rickmansworth D 49 4
Melton Constable to Yarmouth Bch E031
Midhurst - Branch Lines of E 78 9
Midhurst - Branch Lines to F 00 0
Minehead - Branch Line to A 80 2
Mitcham Junction Lines B 01 5
Mitchell & company C 59 8
Monmouth - Branch Lines to E 20 8
Monmouthshire Eastern Valleys D 71 5
Moretonhampstead - BL to C 27 7
Moreton-in-Marsh to Worcester D 26 5
Mountain Ash to Neath D 80 7
N
Newbury to Westbury C 66 6
Newcastle to Hexham D 69 2
Newport (IOW) - Branch Lines to A 26 0
Newquay - Branch Lines to C 71 0
Newton Abbot to Plymouth C 60 4
Newtown to Aberystwyth E 41 3
North East German NG D 44 9
Northern Alpine Narrow Gauge F 37 6
Northern France Narrow Gauge C 75 8
Northern Spain Narrow Gauge E 83 3
North London Line B 94 7
North Woolwich - BLs around C 65 9
Nottingham to Lincoln F 43 7
O
Ongar - Branch Line to E 05 5
Orpington to Tonbridge B 03 9
Oswestry - Branch Lines around E 60 4
Oswestry to Whitchurch E 81 9
Oxford to Bletchley D 57 9
Oxford to Moreton-in-Marsh D 15 9
P
Paddington to Ealing C 37 6
Paddington to Princes Risborough C819
Padstow - Branch Line to B 54 1
Pembroke and Cardigan - BLs to F 29 1
Peterborough to Kings Lynn E 32 1
Plymouth - BLs around B 98 5
Plymouth to St. Austell C 63 5
Pontypool to Mountain Ash D 65 4
Pontypridd to Merthyr F 14 7
Pontypridd to Port Talbot E 86 4
Porthmadog 1954-94 - BLa B 31 2
Portmadoc 1923-46 - BLa B 13 8
Portsmouth to Southampton A 31 4
Portugal Narrow Gauge E 67 3
Potters Bar to Cambridge D 70 8
Princes Risborough - BL to D 05 0
Princes Risborough to Banbury C 85 7
R
Reading to Basingstoke B 27 5
Reading to Didcot C 79 6
Reading to Guildford A 47 5
Redhill to Ashford A 73 4
Return to Blaenau 1970-82 C 64 2
Rhyl to Bangor F 15 4
Rhymney & New Tredegar Lines E 48 2
Rickmansworth to Aylesbury D 61 6
Romania & Bulgaria NG E 23 9
Romneyrail C 32 1
Ross-on-Wye - BLs around E 30 7
Ruabon to Barmouth E 84 0
Rugby to Birmingham E 37 6
Rugby to Loughborough F 12 3
Rugby to Stafford F 07 9
Ryde to Ventnor A 19 2
S
Salisbury to Westbury B 39 8
Saxmundham to Yarmouth C 69 7
Saxony Narrow Gauge D 47 0
Seaton & Sidmouth - BLs to A 95 6
Selsey - Branch Line to A 04 8
Sheerness - Branch Line to B 16 2
Shenfield to Ipswich E 96 3
Shrewsbury - Branch Line to A 86 4
Shrewsbury to Chester E 70 3
Shrewsbury to Crewe F 48 2
Shrewsbury to Ludlow E 21 5
Shrewsbury to Newtown E 29 1
Sierra Leone Narrow Gauge D 28 9
Sirhowy Valley Line E 12 3
Sittingbourne to Ramsgate A 90 1
Slough to Newbury C 56 7
South African Two-foot gauge E 51 2
Southampton to Bournemouth A 42 0
Southend & Southminster BLs E 76 5
Southern Alpine Narrow Gauge F 22 2
Southern France Narrow Gauge C 47 5
South London Line B 46 6
South Lynn to Norwich City F 03 1
Southwold - Branch Line to A 15 4
Spalding - Branch Lines around E 52 9
Stafford to Chester F 34 5
St Albans to Bedford D 08 1
St. Austell to Penzance C 67 3
St. Boswell to Berrick F 44 4
Steaming Through Isle of Wight A
Steaming Through West Hants A 6
Stourbridge to Wolverhampton E
St. Pancras to Barking D 68 5
St. Pancras to Folkestone E 88 8
St. Pancras to St. Albans C 78 9
Stratford-u-Avon to Birmingham D
Stratford-u-Avon to Cheltenham C
Sudbury - Branch Lines to F 19 2
Surrey Narrow Gauge C 87 1
Sussex Narrow Gauge C 68 0
Swanley to Ashford B 45 9
Swansea - Branch Lines around F
Swansea to Carmarthen E 59 8
Swindon to Bristol C 96 3
Swindon to Gloucester D 46 3
Swindon to Newport D 30 2
Swiss Narrow Gauge C 94 9
T
Talyllyn 60 E 98 7
Taunton to Barnstaple B 60 2
Taunton to Exeter C 82 6
Taunton to Minehead F 39 0
Tavistock to Plymouth B 88 6
Tenterden - Branch Line to A 21 5
Three Bridges to Brighton A 35 2
Tilbury Loop C 86 4
Tiverton - BLs around C 62 8
Tivetshall to Beccles D 41 8
Tonbridge to Hastings A 44 4
Torrington - Branch Lines to B 37
Towcester - BLs around E 39 0
Tunbridge Wells BLs A 32 1
U
Upwell - Branch Line to B 64 0
V
Victoria to Bromley South A 98 7
Victoria to East Croydon A 40 6
Vivarais Revisited E 08 6
W
Walsall Routes F 45 1
Wantage - Branch Line to D 25 8
Wareham to Swanage 50 yrs D098
Waterloo to Windsor A 54 3
Waterloo to Woking A 38 3
Watford to Leighton Buzzard D 45
Welshpool to Llanfair E 49 9
Wenford Bridge to Fowey C 09 3
Westbury to Bath B 55 8
Westbury to Taunton C 76 5
West Cornwall Mineral Rlys D 48 7
West Croydon to Epsom B 08 4
West German Narrow Gauge D 93
West London - BLs of C 50 5
West London Line B 84 8
West Wiltshire - BLs of D 12 8
Weymouth - BLs A 65 9
Willesden Jn to Richmond B 71 8
Wimbledon to Beckenham C 58 1
Wimbledon to Epsom B 62 6
Wimborne - BLs around A 97 0
Wisbech - BLs around C 01 7
Witham & Kelvedon - BLs a E 82 6
Woking to Alton A 59 8
Woking to Portsmouth A 25 3
Woking to Southampton A 55 0
Wolverhampton to Shrewsbury E44
Worcester to Birmingham D 97 5
Worcester to Hereford D 38 8
Worthing to Chichester A 06 2
Wrexham to New Brighton F 47 5
Wroxham - BLs around F 31 4
Y
Yeovil - 50 yrs change C 38 3
Yeovil to Dorchester A 76 5
Yeovil to Exeter A 91 8
York to Scarborough F 23 9